SHENANDOAH UNIVERSITY LIBRARY
WINCHESTER, VA 22601

D0084715

TRANSFORMED JUDGMENT

SHENANDOAH UNIV. LIBRARY
WINCHESTER, VA. 22601

© 1990 by
University of Notre Dame Press
Notre Dame, Indiana 46556
All Rights Reserved
Manufactured in the United States of America

Library of Congress Cataloging-in-Publication Data

Jones, L. Gregory.
  Transformed judgment : toward a Trinitarian account of the
moral life / L. Gregory Jones.
    p. cm.
  Includes index.
  ISBN 0-268-01872-3
  1. Christian ethics. 2. Trinity. I. Title.
BJ1251.J62   1990
241—dc20   89-40755
                                                            CIP

BJ   Jones, L. Gregory.
1251
.J62   Transformed judgment
1990

  241 J72t

To the Memory of my Father
S. Jameson Jones, Jr.

ACKNOWLEDGMENTS

One of the central themes of this book is the way in which friends help to form the judgments we learn to make, and I have been blessed with many such friends. Stanley Hauerwas has been both mentor and friend, and my debt to him is incalculable. His range of knowledge and his penetrating insights have saved me from many errors and have helped to shape my argument; his humor and unfailing generosity have given me perspective and encouragement when they were most needed. He is known for spending an extraordinary amount of time with graduate students; in my case, he exceeded even his considerable reputation. Since my move to Baltimore, he has remained a trusted teacher and advisor, and more importantly, a close friend.

I am also fortunate to have had as teachers, advisors, and friends such people as Dennis Campbell, Tom Langford, Moody Smith, Tom Spragens, Ken Surin, and Geoffrey Wainwright. They have contributed much not only to this book but also to my life.

I am indebted to a variety of friends who read part or all of this manuscript at various stages: Jim Buckley, Michael Cartwright, Stephen Fowl, Russ Hittinger, Gil Meilaender, John Milbank, Charlie Pinches, Jeff Powell, Jeff Stout, and Terry Tilley. Their extensive comments and criticisms sharpened my conception of the book and the arguments contained therein. In particular, Jim Buckley, Russ Hittinger, and Jeff Stout made insightful suggestions about the overall argument that enabled me to see more clearly how it should be structured.

I am grateful for the assistance of a number of institutions for their support. The Graduate School of Duke University, the Foundation for Theological Education, and the Andrew Mellon Foundation all provided me with fellowships which relieved my family and me of financial worries during the time of my graduate education. More importantly, I am grateful to the people behind those institutions who give so much time and energy toward providing aid for graduate education.

People at Loyola College, the institution where I now teach, have been both hospitable and helpful. I am fortunate to have a supportive Dean in David Roswell and an extraordinary chairperson in Jim Buckley. Even more, the members of the Department of Theology have made the activity of teaching and writing a more enjoyable enterprise than I could have ever imagined.

I am also grateful to Jim Langford and the people at Notre Dame Press for their help in making this book possible. I am particularly indebted to my editor, Carole Roos, whose careful attention to both style and substance has significantly helped this book be more readable.

The debt I owe my wife cannot be measured. She has pushed when I needed to be pushed, encouraged me when I needed encouragement, graciously assumed tasks that I should have been doing so that more time could be given to writing, and she has put up with me with good humor and sensitivity. Her vocation as a parish minister continually reminds me that writing theology is not of much significance unless it has some bearing on the lives of people and their particular needs and hopes, joys and griefs. Perhaps most importantly, however, my wife's life is an example to me and reminds me how much I need to be transformed if I hope to become a person of character.

Our son Nathan is the source of great joy. He helps to remind me, sometimes rather insistently, that there are many things more important than writing a book or even reading one. I am also thankful for the support of my mother, her new husband, and my sisters and brother and their families. They have helped me to understand what things I ought to care about.

The book is dedicated to the memory of my father, who died unexpectedly the summer before I began my divinity school education. It was he who instilled in me a love both for God and for scholarship, and in his friendship I have learned, grown, and seen the world and my own life more clearly. His life would not have made sense except as a reflection of his belief in the God of Jesus Christ, and that life stands as an example of the kind of character to which I aspire and for which I pray. For his life and for his friendship, I thank God.

L. Gregory Jones

July 1989

INTRODUCTION

ETHICS AND THE CHARACTER
OF MORAL JUDGMENT

Over the past decade or so several prominent philosophers and theologians have returned the virtues to a
significant place in moral reflection, arguing in particular that any coherent account of moral judgment requires as its central focus an understanding of how a
person's character affects and shapes the judgment that
is made. Indeed, were it not for the fact that accounts
of the virtues and their connection to moral judgment
have an illustrious history going back to Plato and Aristotle, it would appear that virtue theories simply represent the latest (soon-to-be-passing) fad. After all, like
many fads, interest in the virtues emerged with a relatively sudden flash, generated heated opposition, and
tended to degenerate into rather boring debates.

But there is more to the (re)turn to the virtues than
the sterility of the recent debates might lead one to
suspect. Virtue theorists have acknowledged the importance of rules, and many moral philosophers have
acknowledged virtue and character as legitimate topics
for moral reflection and for understanding the activity
of moral judgment. Thus the primary focus should not
be on asking, Is there a necessary place for the virtues
within ethical reflection? but rather, What kind of account of the virtues and of moral judgment, of all the
possible options, should be developed?

In this book I attempt to sketch an answer to the latter

1

question by arguing that the most coherent account of moral judgment is one grounded in, and lived in relation to the mystery of the Triune God. Such a claim is bound to appear odd to many, if not most, readers for it suggests either a kind of pious concern that does not do any work intellectually or an unwarranted attempt to sneak theology into moral reflection.

I am sympathetic to those worries for I am not interested in any attempts either to appeal to piety instead of argument or to sneak theology in the back door. However, I am convinced that an adequate understanding of how the virtues are acquired and character is formed reveals that theological (or, for that matter, antitheological or atheological) claims about such matters as God, the world, and life and death make a decisive difference for how the activity of moral judgment is construed.

My argument is developed in three chapters. First, I argue that the activity of moral judgment is inextricably tied to particular social contexts and is decisively affected by the presence or absence of theological convictions of one sort or another. Drawing on arguments from the philosophy of language as well as moral philosophy, I suggest that people *learn* to describe their actions and lives in one way rather than another, and that people *learn* to acquire and exercise the virtues ingredient in making wise judgments. Such learning occurs in and through the social contexts of particular linguistic communities. I contend that what matters is not simply the existence of linguistic communities, but the fact that these communities are connected to particular theological (or antitheological or atheological) views.

Consequently moral descriptions and accounts of the virtues vary (to one degree or another) among such communities, and the shape of moral judgment will likewise vary. Thus an account of moral judgment requires a correlative account of a theologically specified tradition, and, consequently, it is important to attend to the ways a person is inducted into, and formed in, such a tradition.

In the second and third chapters, I discuss such induction and formation from the standpoint of the Christian tradition's view that human beings are to live in relation to the mystery of the Triune God. Because I am convinced that the depiction of God as Triune is central to the most coherent and truthful account of moral judgment and the moral life that can be offered, I attempt to show how (at least one version of) that depiction provides the context for understanding the specific kinds of friendships and specific kinds of practices necessary if a person is to become capable of making wise moral judgments.

In the second chapter I provide a brief sketch of what I mean by "the mystery of the Triune God," and then outline the understanding of "personhood" that is correlative to the depiction of God as Triune. On this view, becoming a person involves the struggle of learning to live in relation to others—paradigmatically the other who is the Triune God. Because the production of personhood requires *learning* to be in relation, it is important to specify how friendships and practices as central contexts in which such learning takes place are related. I argue in particular that the primary friendship which a person ought to have is with the Triune God who has befriended humanity in Jesus Christ. Such friendship calls forth a life of transformative discipleship which is learned in and through the friendships and practices of Christian communities.

Contrary to some conceptions of the moral life, I contend that discipleship is neither a linear and stable process of ongoing growth nor an oppositional dualism of before and after some dramatic turning such as conversion. While I argue that the moral life should receive its decisive specification in the person and work of Jesus

Christ, I also contend that it is a mistake to assume that the moral life should be understood exclusively as a matter of following Jesus. Instead, the moral life, understood most adequately in terms of Christian life, should be lived in the mystery of the Triune God. From such a perspective, I suggest that the moral life involves an ongoing "perichoretic dance." Such a dance, grounded in the perichoretic relations of God's Trinity, requires and enables people to discern the overall pattern their lives are to take, to puzzle with others about what that patterning entails concretely, and to question received claims to truth from the standpoint of the Gospel.

In the third chapter I discuss the friendships and practices of Christian communities. It is in and through such friendships and practices that persons are produced and given their specific shape. I briefly indicate the ways in which the doctrine of God's Trinity entails a specific understanding of the shape and pattern of Christian community and then outline more precisely the contours of the Christian life that is formed and transformed in and through particular friendships and practices in friendship with God. I focus particularly on the relationships between Christian practices and Christian community and on the ways in which friendships and practices serve as pedagogies of discipleship.

The central claim is that, from the standpoint of the Christian tradition, the moral life requires not only formation but *trans*formation in moral judgment. The moral life is inextricably tied to responsive friendship with the Triune God and is enabled by such Christian practices as baptism, eucharist, forgiveness-reconciliation, and the interpretation of Scripture. Central to Christian convictions is the belief that it is an exceedingly difficult task to see and describe the world rightly and to think, feel, and act well. Accomplishing such a task requires a willingness to have one's life formed and transformed by the mystery of the Triune God.

The second and third chapters are, as they stand, radically incomplete. I offer no more than a sketch of a trinitarian account of the moral life, and even less of a trinitarian account of moral judgment or the formation and transformation necessary for moral judgment. I do not display here the substantive difference a trinitarian perspective brings to various issues and often vexing problems, though I am convinced that it does make such a difference. Even so, I hope my argument clearly indicates how and why theological, antitheological, or atheological claims are crucial to an account of the moral life and the formation *of* moral judgments by showing the way an account of friendship with God and the friendships and practices of Christian communities provide a distinctive shape to formation and transformation *in* moral judgment.

Accounts which fail to recognize the difference theological claims make for ethics must be judged to be deficient. Such deficiencies arise in more than one way, as can be seen by a brief exposition of the views of three thinkers—Edmund Pincoffs, Martha Nussbaum, and Stanley Hauerwas—who have provided accounts of moral judgment and the virtues. Though their views are in some ways similar to my own, and though I have learned much from them in developing the argument of this book, ultimately each of their accounts is deficient for its failure to attend to the ways in which theological claims make a decisive difference for ethics and in particular for an account of moral judgment.

In his book *Quandaries and Virtues,* Edmund Pincoffs criticizes those who "reduce" ethics and moral judgment to the resolution of quandaries, arguing instead that the primary concern of ethics ought to be with qualities of character, with the virtues and the vices. Pincoffs believes that moral character and moral judgment are intimately bound together; as he puts it, "Moral judgment is an expression of the character of the person who offers it."[1] Hence Pincoffs and I are allies against views which attempt to exclude questions of character and the virtues from an account of moral judgment.

Pincoffs wants to spell out his account of character and the virtues on the basis of what it means to be human. He states that his perspective can "only be understood against a background of assumed facts about the common life of human beings,"[2] a claim which reflects his belief that humans are social beings, that social life is necessary for the presence of characteristic human qualities. Thus Pincoffs argues that those qualities necessary for the maintenance and flourishing of human life will be ingredient in any account of the virtues. Though "as tendencies within the common life or within the organization of common life change through history or across cultures" there may be differences in what counts as a virtue or a vice, Pincoffs argues that such virtues as justice, persistence, courage, and honesty are likely to be found in any situations in which human well-being is not frustrated.[3]

Pincoffs contends that attention to the "common life" of human beings is sufficient to provide an account of the virtues, explicitly rejecting the familiar claim that such an account requires a teleological perspective. As he describes it, "the virtues of persons and actions are qualities of their working well. But we do not need to know some supervenient common end before we can distinguish good from bad working." He goes on to claim that the virtues and vices "have to do with the good for man only in the sense that, given the goods that men tend to pursue, these qualities are desirable ones."[4] In short, Pincoffs offers a functionalist account of the virtues.

On his account, theological views are unimportant. As he puts it, "learning to be the right sort and doing what the teacher can to help that learning are not tied to any particular theological opinions. . . . A just man is a just man is a just man."[5] While I agree that there is a genuine virtue called "justice," I claim that the genuine virtue requires theological specification in a way that Pincoffs does not. It requires such specification because there are other accounts of what "justice" is which, from a theological perspective, are either wrong or at best simulacra of the genuine virtue. Pincoffs mistakenly assumes that because different accounts of the virtues include something called "justice" or "courage," those different accounts are recommending the same kinds of dispositions and/or the same kinds of activities—when in fact they are not, or at least often are not.

Alasdair MacIntyre makes a related point against Pincoffs when he argues that there are different accounts of the virtues and that what is meant by a virtue cannot be discerned by referring to the "common life." According to MacIntyre, it is possible to recognize a state of affairs in which "there is a socially and politically determinate form of common life, that within that common life certain persons and perhaps groups exhibit genuine virtues and that, just insofar as those persons and groups exhibit these virtues, they are put in conflict with the forms of the common life in serious and long-term ways."[6] Thus any account of the virtues that has been specified with sufficient adequacy to provide guidance for moral practice and moral education will be functional within some forms of social and political life and dysfunctional in others.[7] There will be, and have been, social orders in which to embody the genuine virtue of justice (as I would argue for it theologically) is to put oneself at odds with the "common life" of one's culture *and* that culture's understanding of justice.

Pincoffs's rejection of a teleological view entails a rejection of at least some depictions of God. The issue of *telos* does not simply concern the individual's "supervenient end" or even the directedness of particular social contexts, though such claims are not irrelevant. More determinatively, at least on the view I will defend, the *telos* is a way of characterizing the God who is the end and goal of human life.

Thus theological claims, and the forms of social and political life necessary for their embodiment, do make a difference for an account of the virtues and moral judgment. What counts for "justice" or "courage" often diverges in significant ways in different accounts of the virtues. Of course Pincoffs might well retort that despite these arguments he has *in fact* delineated a compelling list of the virtues independently of any theological views or any social contexts.

Taken on his own terms, however, Pincoffs does not succeed in so doing. For example, he lists "forgivingness" as a nonmandatory moral virtue. But for Christians such a quality is a mandatory moral virtue, and for Aristotle grounds can be given for thinking it a vice. Humility, patience, and hopefulness are arguably central Christian virtues which do not appear in Pincoffs's list, and his mandatory moral virtue of "nonbelligerence" is neither strong enough for (at least some) versions of the Christian virtue of "peaceableness" nor explicit enough to explain why some thinkers have argued that belligerence is sometimes morally justified and mandated.

In short, Pincoffs's position is not context-independent; though he would probably dispute the claim, it is dependent on the social context of (at least one version of) twentieth-century liberal democratic theory and its correlative presumption that theological views are irrelevant to moral discussion. I have already suggested ways in which his account would be unacceptable to either an Aristotelian or a Christian account—perhaps even more revealing is his claim that "Saint Francis of Assisi is a moral model of only limited relevance; it is hard to reconcile true selflessness with self-respect and dignity, which are also qualities that provide reasons for preference...."[8] On such an account, many persons often identified by theological accounts as persons of virtue—for example, within the Christian tradition, Mother Teresa or perhaps even Jesus—are of only limited relevance.

I am not arguing, at least on this point, that the content of Pincoffs's position is wrong. The differences in our accounts of moral education, moral judgment, and the virtues will become more clear later. What I am contending here is that Pincoffs's position fails as an attempt to provide a context-independent account of the virtues—that his position is deficient precisely because it fails to recognize the difference that theological views make.

In contrast to Pincoffs's, Martha Nussbaum's views are more complex. While she ultimately appeals to something like Pincoffs's "common life of human beings," she is also an Aristotelian and her views are closely tied to the rejection of other accounts of the virtues and a vindication of an Aristotelian account. Indeed her work on Aristotle is impressive and has been influential, and she has done a great deal toward returning accounts of moral education, moral judgment, and the virtues to a prominent place in ethics. Even so, in a manner both similar to and different from Pincoffs's, her constructive argument fails adequately to recognize the ways in which theological (or antitheological or atheological) claims affect an account of the virtues and the moral life.

In *The Fragility of Goodness* Nussbaum notes that Stoic and Christian views about such matters as divine providence and the relationship between human goodness and divine grace significantly alter the way in which certain questions are put as well as the answers given to them.[9] In addition, Nussbaum has argued that Samuel Beckett's novels exhibit the conviction that

Christian emotions are wrong and thus must be "un-written" before an alternative set of emotions can be written.[10] She has recognized, in a way Pincoffs does not, that humility is central to a Christian account of the virtues, while it is not for an Aristotelian account.[11] Thus it would appear that Nussbaum thinks that Christian accounts of the moral life entail commitments that are in some ways quite different from and at odds with an Aristotelian account.

That Nussbaum recognizes the significance of theological, antitheological, or atheological claims is shown in her criticism of Aristotle as well as of other past writers on virtue. She claims that they "lacked sensitivity to the ways in which different traditions of discourse, different conceptual schemes, articulate the world, and also to the profound connections between the structure of discourse and the structure of experience itself."[12] Even so, the way in which Nussbaum specifies the differences and disagreements among these diverse "traditions of discourse" reveals a deficiency in her approach. In order to understand the problem it is necessary to spell out in greater detail her argument in "Non-Relative Virtues: An Aristotelian Approach."

Nussbaum's argument is structured around an attempt to show that "relativist" accounts of the virtues are wrong, that a universally true account of human morality and the virtues can be found. Early in the essay she sets up the contrast in terms of transcultural norms, which are justifiable with reference to reasons of universal human validity, and norms that are local both in origin and application.[13]

Nussbaum argues that on an Aristotelian approach there are spheres of experience and choice which are universal in scope, and virtues are whatever it is to choose appropriately in each sphere of experience. She recognizes that people will disagree about what the appropriate ways of acting and reacting in fact *are*, but that, as Aristotle sets things up, "they are arguing about the same thing, and advancing competing specifications of the same virtue."[14] Thus when Nussbaum discusses the fact that humility is a virtue for Christians but not for Aristotelians, she contends that the dispute amounts to rival accounts of one and the same thing; as she puts it, "Christian humility would be a rival specification of the same virtue whose Greek specification is given in Aristotle's account of *megalopsuchia*, namely, the proper way to behave toward the question of one's own worth."[15]

Nussbaum anticipates some objections to her approach, but her responses do little more than shift the force of the objections. My concern is not so much with the objections she anticipates but with two deeper problems in the structure of her argument.

The first problem is that she sets up the alternatives as a choice between the local and the universal. Nussbaum thinks that if someone rejects the claim that there are "trans-cultural norms, justifiable with reference to reasons of universal human validity, with reference to which we may appropriately criticize different local conceptions of the good," the result is relativism.[16] Thus when she refers to nonuniversal accounts of the moral life, she consistently writes in terms of "local" traditions, conceptions of the good, and the like. She describes such nonuniversal accounts as being *"simply* a reflection of local traditions and values," and that proponents of such accounts are *"just* narrating a different tradition" rather than arguing about what is good or right.[17]

Such false alternatives set up her relativist opponent as a straw-man. Accounts of the moral life are grounded in socially embodied traditions which nonetheless claim to be true and are indeed concerned with arguments about what is good and right. Nussbaum might agree, only noting that what I fail to recognize are the "features of humanness that lie beneath all local traditions"[18] which make it possible to be objective and to offer a universally binding account of the moral life. Insofar as "features of humanness" means simply that people in diverse traditions and social contexts have enough in common to make argument and criticism possible and even necessary, I have no quarrel with Nussbaum. Defending the possibility of argument and criticism across cultures and traditions seems to be a significant concern for Nussbaum, arising out of the fact that her imagined opponent is someone who thinks it is not possible to criticize conceptions of the good outside of "local" arrangements. Once the choices are not confined to the universalist or the relativist, however, and are seen in the context of diverse and competing conceptions of the good grounded in socially embodied traditions, Nussbaum's worry appears misplaced.

Nussbaum may argue that I still have failed to recognize the shared features of humanness which make non-context-dependent objectivity possible. In response I first question Nussbaum's notion of an objective, universal standpoint. Here reference to Nussbaum's rhetoric is relevant, for in discussing the "objective" criticism her position affords she makes reference to the inclusive "we" and "our." So she says that the relativist has not shown why "*we* could not, at the end of the day, say that certain ways of conceptualizing death are more in keeping with the totality of *our* evidence and with the totality of *our* wishes for flourishing life than others. . . ."[19] Or she says with reference to Foucault's discussion of the history of sexual ideas that certain ways the Western contemporary debate on these matters has been organized (as a result of some combination of Christian morality with nineteenth-century pseudo-science) are "especially silly, arbitrary, and limiting, inimical to a human search for flourishing." Thus Foucault's account provides "not only a sign that someone once thought differently, but also that it is possible for *us* to think differently."[20]

Curiously, however, Nussbaum never stops to consider how parochial such references to "we" and "our" and "us" really are. Who constitutes such a "we" that has come to agreement on what the evidence is and what our wishes for a flourishing life are? Sexuality is obviously a difficult area to understand and to discuss, but from what standpoint does she assume that all of "us" *want* to think differently? It appears that Nussbaum's so-called inclusive, objective, and universal account actually turns on a rather parochial definition of who counts and who has agreement in a way that eliminates, rather than encourages, the possibility for criticism and argument.

The second deeper problem with Nussbaum's approach is the way in which her argument is structured to provide those shared features of humanness. I do not propose to concentrate my objection on her list of shared features,[21] for I have already indicated that people in diverse cultures and traditions have enough in common to make argument and criticism across those cultures and traditions possible and even necessary. Rather the deeper problem with Nussbaum's account is her assumption that the virtues are correlative to relatively autonomous spheres of choice and universal experience, which constitute the shared features of humanness. It may be interesting to chart out lists like she does, but it does not lead to the conclusion that there is a *single* debate about what virtue is appropriate for a particular "sphere of experience." The virtues are interrelated and are grounded in particular patterns of belief and are acquired in and through specific friendships and practices, such that the disagreement between a Christian and an Aristotelian about humility is not simply a disagreement about the proper attitude toward one's own self-worth. Rather that disagreement is much broader and is intimately connected to the fact that the Aristotelian and the Christian have divergent theological judgments. Those features of humanness such as death or the body, which all people "share" in one sense, do not provide a universal or "objective" way to characterize the moral life. Christian convictions about self-worth, death, and the body are interrelated and must be seen in relation to particular theologically derived practices and patterns of belief.

Thus when Nussbaum suggests that "if we should succeed in ruling out conceptions of the proper attitude to one's own human worth that are based on a notion of original sin, that would be a moral work of enormous significance,"[22] she misunderstands the significance of the Christian understanding of original sin. It is not simply a claim about the proper attitude to one's own human worth; it is bound up with much larger claims about who God is and what the world is like. From the perspective of a Christian such as myself, the only way in which such a ruling out of (a properly specified, not poorly understood, conception of) original sin as relevant to the moral life and the delineation of the virtues could be acceptable would be if Christian claims about the God of Jesus Christ were decisively shown to be wrong. That is to say, "original sin" is not an empirical claim about human self-worth; rather it is a claim rooted in the recognition that when faced with Christ's salvation humanity discovers that it would rather live apart from, than in relation to God.

Thus Nussbaum's account is deficient because it fails to recognize the ways in which theological claims affect the account given of the moral life. Insofar as Aristotelians and Christians argue about how life should be lived, it will not be by isolating questions about the proper attitude to one's own worth; it can only be done with reference to the whole scope of friendships, practices, and patterns of belief which are intimately connected to judgments about God, the world, and life and death.

Those who know Stanley Hauerwas's work will undoubtedly find it odd for me to suggest that his account is deficient for its failure to recognize how theological, antitheological, or atheological claims affect the account given of the moral life. After all, Hauerwas has been at the forefront of the return of character and the virtues to ethical reflection. In addition, he has been one of the most influential thinkers who has insisted that theological convictions make a difference to ethics, insisting in particular that theological convictions must be socially embodied if they are to have any force or are to be judged truthful. His arguments are not susceptible to the kinds of criticisms I have made of Pincoffs and Nussbaum, for he recognizes that theological convictions matter in a way that neither Pincoffs nor Nussbaum does. Why, then, is his account deficient?

There is a disjunction between Hauerwas's emphasis on character and the virtues on the one hand and his arguments about the importance of theological commitments on the other. He has not adequately explained how the account of character, the virtues, and moral education he wants to offer is tied to the theological claims he makes about the God of Jesus Christ. It is not easy to spell out this disjunction, for Hauerwas's position has been developing over a number of years through the publication of a wide variety and large number of occasional essays. Thus it is important to chart some of the developments in Hauerwas's thought in order to specify exactly why I think there is such a disjunction.

Hauerwas's dissertation, published in revised form as *Character and the Christian Life,* is an attempt to connect the themes of character and the virtues to an account of Christian life. Though Hauerwas concludes the book with the observation that those "who are loyal to God's act in Jesus Christ cannot think unimportant the way we as agents act and the kind of persons we become as a result,"[23] his account of character is too formal and thus lacks theological specificity. He develops an account of character from Aristotle and the philosophical arguments of Aquinas and then applies that account to a theological understanding of sanctification. Hauerwas sees the relation in terms of "retranslating" themes associated with sanctification into terms of the formation of character,[24] suggesting that though the substance of a philosophical (e.g., Aristotelian) and a theological (e.g., Christian) account of character may differ, the structure of an account of character is basically the same for each.

Hauerwas continues that presumption in two essays in *A Community of Character*, published some seven years later. His essay "The Virtues and Our Communities: Human Nature as History" is basically a philosophical explication of virtue, the virtues, and their relation to the histories of particular communities.[25] In the following essay, "Character, Narrative, and Growth in the Christian Life," Hauerwas applies his account of character to Christian life. He does note that such theological notions as conversion alter the basic presumptions about moral "development," but the bulk of the essay is little more than an application of a philosophical account of character and the virtues to a theological understanding of Christian life.[26]

Over the same period as he was developing his arguments about character, however, Hauerwas had been developing a theological account of the centrality of Jesus for Christian ethics. In other essays found in *A Community of Character*, Hauerwas argues that Christian life must be construed in terms of discipleship, that it is only by becoming a disciple of Jesus that people can understand the truth about human existence. More particularly, he argues that becoming a disciple means being incorporated into Jesus' story by becoming a part of the Church, that community called into being by Jesus Christ and formed according to the biblical texts that bear witness to Jesus Christ.[27] In those essays there is reference to particular virtues and to the Church as a school for virtue, but the themes of character and virtue are not prominent.

In *The Peaceable Kingdom*,[28] his only book-length argument since *Character and the Christian Life*, Hauerwas attempts to unite the emphasis on character with his theological convictions. Thus there is a more explicit discussion about the importance of sin to an account of the moral life, and he devotes a chapter each to character, to community as the context for the formation of character, and to the significance of Jesus. Hauerwas's analysis and arguments are often powerful and insightful, but even here the themes are not adequately explicated in relation to each other.

The deficiency occurs in two interrelated though distinct ways. On the one hand, his discussion still tends to be too "bilingual"; talk of character and the virtues here, then talk of sin and grace and discipleship and Jesus there, without carefully working out whether and how those vocabularies are related to each other. While Hauerwas's rhetoric sometimes ties the language of character and the virtues to an account of Christian life, he has not shown materially what difference it makes. In this sense, Hauerwas's account is deficient because it is incomplete, and making it more complete would require considerably revising his understanding of the relationship between theological convictions and an account of the moral life.

For example, Hauerwas's account tends to place too much emphasis on the continuity of character as necessary for Christian life. When Hauerwas writes about sin as self-deception and the ways in which confrontation with the cross reveals how much humanity hates God, his insights are rich and his arguments compelling. But it is difficult to square such emphases with the ways in which Hauerwas writes about the continuity and stability which a person of character possesses. Hauerwas at times locates continuity in the "self" rather than in the God who continually calls people's "selves" into question. Put in the terms which I develop in the third chapter, Hauerwas's discussions of character tend to underestimate the necessity of ongoing questioning and puzzlement which is central to life lived in relation to the mystery of the Triune God.

Such a claim points to a second way in which Hauerwas's account is deficient, namely that he has failed to explicate the relationship between a Christian depiction of God as Triune and an account of the moral life. Providing such an explication would be one way to resolve the first problem, for he could show how a particular way of construing God as Triune would bring together the kinds of philosophical and theological issues with which he has been concerned. But Hauerwas has not shown *theologically* how his christological claims are related to the other persons of the Trinity, in particular to an account of the work of the Holy Spirit in creating and sustaining the friendships and practices which enable people's lives to be (re)shaped and (trans)formed.

The incompleteness of Hauerwas's account lies in his tendency to focus his account so exclusively on Jesus that he fails to articulate adequately how Christian life is shaped by the mystery of the Triune God. His account of the moral life is christologically shaped, but it needs to be "trinitarianly" shaped.[29]

Thus, ultimately, Hauerwas's perspective is deficient in articulating the ways in which theological claims affect an account of the moral life, albeit for different reasons than either Pincoffs's or Nussbaum's. While I have argued that all three of their accounts are deficient methodologically, I have not provided any kind of sustained argument to show how or why their substantive accounts are thereby inadequate and/or wrong. The divergences between each of their accounts and my own will become more apparent as the argument proceeds.

It may appear odd that, given my insistence on the decisive impact theological claims make both methodologically and substantively, the first chapter of the book is more philosophical than theological. The kind of case I want to make for the centrality of a depiction of God as Triune for the moral life and an account of moral judgment requires attention to these kinds of philosophical issues. However, theological claims will be involved both in the way the arguments are constructed and in the substance of the proposals. Even so, the ultimate vindication of those arguments will not come until the second and third chapters.

Even though I likely raise more questions and issues in this book than I answer and address, I hope that the book points in some important directions. For those who reject the Christian account of God as Triune, those directions may be toward more adequate specifications of disagreements. For those who accept the Christian account but want to specify it in different ways, those directions may be toward further and more complete explorations of the centrality of the Triune God for an account of the moral life. If this book can help to serve as such a pointer, I will be content.

1. LEARNING TO DESCRIBE ACTIONS, PERSONS, AND THE WORLD

SOCIAL CONTEXTS AND MORAL JUDGMENT

One of the central issues in an account of the moral life is how to understand the relationship between actions and the persons who perform those actions. One way to deal with such a question is to deny that there is a relevant relationship. On such a view, it is assumed that the proper domain of moral thought is the making of moral judgments about specific actions and practices independently of the persons involved in the actions and practices. There is no essential relationship between acts and agents, for acts can be characterized and evaluated without reference to the character of the agents. The agent's perspective may be important in what is actually done, but that is a matter left to psychologists and sociologists. It is not involved in the making of moral judgments.

If there is no relevant relationship between acts and the persons who perform them, then the descriptions of actions are understood to be noncontroversial. The situation lies wholly "out there"; there is agreement on the "facts" even if there is disagreement about those facts' relation to "values." Disputes over facts and values have often been divided into two schools of thought. On the one hand, philosophers such as R. M. Hare have argued that fact is logically distinct from value, and that thus there is no logical inconsistency in denying a value judgment even if one has assented to the facts brought in support of the judgment. On the other hand, philosophers such as Philippa Foot have argued that certain facts entail within them the truth or falsity of moral beliefs such that assent to the facts requires assent to the value judgments that follow from them. The disagreement between Hare and Foot occurs within a broader agreement about description; they share the view that the description of the "facts" is a relatively noncontroversial matter.[1]

Insofar as descriptions are noncontroversial, moral judgment is an activity essentially unrelated to theological (or antitheological or atheological) convictions. On the strong version of this claim, an account of God has either no role or a deleterious role in moral judgment; such tradition-informed beliefs are to be avoided or overcome in making moral judgments. On the weak version of this claim, such beliefs play a "motivating" role in moral judgment; they do not affect the substance of the judgment, but they are helpful in motivating the agent to make the judgment she should have, and could have, made independently of the beliefs.

Such a cluster of views rests on the mistaken premise that acts and agency can be separated. In response, I will show that moral judgment is an activity through which people give form not only to actions but also to themselves. It is when human life is construed narratively that the inextricable interrelation between acts and agency becomes clear.

But many who recognize that character and moral judgment are interrelated fail to see the ways in which descriptions vary. So Edmund Pincoffs thinks that "a just man is a just man is a just man,"[2] without considering the significantly different ways in which, for example, a Humean and a Christian describe what constitutes a just person or what it would mean to act justly.

He also does not recognize that understanding and/or resolving such divergences would require attention to a complex web of friendships, practices, and beliefs underlying those descriptions.

J. Philip Wogaman, who asserts that theological convictions do matter, fails to recognize that descriptions are controversial. In a review of Stanley Hauerwas's book, *Character and the Christian Life*, Wogaman warns that we should not reduce "all ethics to an analysis of character formation as though we did not have to explore problems and dilemmas on their merits."[3] In the preface to his own book, *A Christian Method of Moral Judgment*, Wogaman writes that "a rounded discussion of virtue and character-formation" is presupposed by his account; but curiously he thinks that his account of the substance of moral judgment does not vary among Christians and non-Christians because "the whole human family occupies common ground in the moral life."[4] Thus according to Wogaman, theological beliefs may affect the "ultimate meaning" of an action, but they are little more than the motivating source of actions; they do not decisively affect the description of actions, persons, and the world.[5]

In contrast, I argue that the description of situations, actions, and lives is a central and controversial matter. Linguistic communities play an important role in providing the resources whereby people describe things in one way rather than another.

In this chapter my argument moves through three stages. In the first stage, I will contrast the "non-agential" characterization of the self and of human action with an "agential" one. Second, I will discuss the social context of description, showing why descriptions vary among linguistic communities. In the third, I will focus on the ways in which theological views are related to social contexts and moral judgment.

1.1 THE SELF, AGENCY, AND ACTION

The characterization of human action is closely tied to judgments about what constitutes the self. The view that there is no relevant connection between human action and the person who performs that action presupposes a particular philosophical psychology. Any adequate challenge to that view will require an accompanying challenge to the understanding of human life which underlies it.

1.11 NON-AGENTIAL VIEWS OF THE SELF AND HUMAN ACTION

A great deal of twentieth-century moral philosophy and theology has tended to model its study of human action and selfhood in accord with scientific explanation. The self is described primarily in terms of what can be observed; hence the importance of what is known as the "observer's standpoint." The self is known through observable actions, plus any psychological, sociological, and physiological data that help to understand what "caused" those actions.

The model of moral theory that attempts to be "scientific" and seeks an "objective" standpoint for the description of action is rooted in a philosophical psychology that goes back to Descartes and Kant. In particular, it is the desire for certainty in the case of Descartes and/or objectivity in the case of Kant that animates this scientific perspective and its philosophical psychology. Anthropocentric (or subjective) properties are to be avoided; instead an account of things in absolute terms and from a neutral, objective perspective is given.

This view also influenced explanations of human behavior. But all such explanations are inherently reductive; by seeking to understand human nature "neutrally" and apart from all "subjective" properties, these explanations exclude self-understanding. What is left is what Charles Taylor calls a "thin theory of the self,"[6] so named because it is a self stripped of subjective properties. This thin theory is deeply attractive to many people because it is modeled on the natural sciences, and since these sciences have had explanatory success, there is a kind of "prestige by association."

But this model of the self is attractive for an even more basic reason—it has a strong moral appeal. It pictures a self which is wholly free and autonomous, capable of achieving a kind of disengagement from the world by objectifying it. Such a view of human agency provides people a strong sense of freedom, dignity, and power. It is, in Taylor's words, a "flattering and inspiring" view. But it is also fundamentally wrongheaded in that it is unable to account for crucial features of human life.

This model of the self underlies diverse and often conflicting theories of human behavior and action. One theory, behaviorism, contends that a person's actions are explicable in terms of certain physical or social conditions or by an appeal to her particular set of dispositions. The behaviorist model denies any fundamental meaning to a notion of an "internal" self, contending instead that a person is basically the product of external forces. In the following passage Clark Hull describes an ideal science of human behavior:

> An ideally adequate theory of even so-called purposive behavior ought, therefore, to begin with colorless movement and mere receptor impulses as such, and from these build up step by step both adaptive and maladaptive behavior. The present approach does not deny the molar reality of purposive acts (as opposed to movement), of intelligence, of insight, of goals, or intents, or strivings, or of value; on the contrary, we insist upon the genuineness of these forms of behavior. We hope

ultimately to show the logical right to the use of such concepts by deducing them as secondary principles from more elementary objective primary principles. Once they have been derived we shall not only understand them better but be able to use them with more detailed effectiveness, particularly in the deduction of the movements which mediate (or fail to mediate) goal attainment, than would be the case if we accepted teleological sequences at the outset as gross, unanalyzed (and unanalyzable) wholes.[7]

Although Hull's ideal is only one version of behaviorism, it represents the goal of explaining and analyzing action on a "scientific" basis which excludes any tendency to "anthropomorphic subjectivism."

The varieties of behaviorism have been subjected to a number of devastating critiques, perhaps most notably Charles Taylor's *The Explanation of Behavior*,[8] for their inability to give an adequate account of the role of intention and purpose in human action. Moreover, behaviorism is closely allied to determinism, and such views do not adequately account for the human capacity for (at least partial) self-determination. Behaviorism does not currently have a great many philosophical defenders, particularly because it limits rather than expands human freedom, dignity, and power. Yet it continues to have power as a reductive characterization of human behavior, and the explanatory significance of behaviorist reductions cannot be excluded *a priori*. The difficulty lies not so much with the reduction, for in principle it is possible that greater explanatory success will be achieved than has heretofore been demonstrated; the real difficulty is the inadequacy of behaviorism's underlying philosophical psychology.

Behaviorism is not the only view of the self which is grounded in an attempt at "objectivity." The dualistic models of the self are a family of views opposed to behaviorism but also predicated on a "scientific" model of the self. They continue to exert a wide philosophical influence and have a hold on the contemporary moral imagination. Such models remain within the domain of "science," but they attempt to overcome behaviorism's weaknesses by accounting for the place of purposes and intentions.

Dualism is specified in such models in a variety of ways, but they all have to do with a sharp philosophical distinction between the "mind" and the "body." Whereas behaviorism is unable to account for purposes and intentions, the dualistic models locate intentions in an "internal" event separate from bodily movement. Actions are bodily movements *plus* some kind of special "mental" event. Actions are distinguished by the kind of cause which brings them about; as Taylor characterizes this view, actions are "events which are peculiar in that they are brought about by desires, or intentions, or combinations of desires and beliefs."[9] Thus *qua* bodily movements, actions resemble other events; what distinguishes them is their inner, "mental" cause.

Given the "scientific" view of the self, human freedom seems to stand or fall with the existence and reality of these "mental causes." If humans do not have such mental machinery, the behaviorist/determinist argues, then they are the product of the interaction of physiological, sociological, and psychological forces. The dualist attempts to demonstrate the reality of such a mental background. Hence the primary disputes within the scientific conception are about whether there are mental faculties (e.g., the will) which can be said to cause human action.

The dualistic model is subject to strong counterarguments. One such argument, powerfully developed by Gilbert Ryle in *The Concept of Mind*,[10] is that the dualistic model is a caricature of what actually happens in human life. The dualistic view implies that every time I act I actually perform two acts rather than one; the observable movement and the internal willing that causes the act. But people do not typically think of human activity in this way. If I decide to take a walk, I do not normally think in terms of an act of will prior to the observable act of walking. Must I "will" to put one leg in front of the other at each moment or can I simply "will" to take a walk and then assume that the movements of my legs are somehow subsumed in that description?

A second argument against the dualist view is that the explication of "internal" causes must be made in terms of their effects. In any genuine causal relation, the cause must be characterized independently from the event, for otherwise it is impossible to know how one causes the effect in the other. It is impossible to describe a volition or an act of will in terms of what it was thought to have caused. For example, it is impossible for me to explain my "will" to move my fork in order to eat without using the notion of my will to move my fork. Hence my willing as such cannot be the cause of my movement because the reference to the fork's movement inheres in the very description of my willing. My "will" is thus not contingently or causally related to my act, but rather is a logical property of it. Hence intention (or motive) and action ought not be understood in terms of cause and effect; they are more closely interrelated.

A third objection to the dualist view is that even on its own terms there is the problem of explaining how I can claim the internal event that causes the act as genuinely mine. To say that something occurred within me when the act was performed does not establish the cause as mine nor does it explain how it is related to the bodily movement. The primary reason the dualist view seems to be a plausible explanation is that people think they need some explanation of action beyond their avowed reasons for acting.

If the dualist model is rejected as inadequate, there

seems to be no other alternative than to accept the behaviorist view, which seems to be even more unsatisfactory. Intuitively, the dualistic view seems closer to being right, for it encompasses motives and intentions in the characterization of human behavior; the behaviorist view appears to be inherently reductive. For this reason many moral philosophers and theologians continue to subscribe to a version of the dualism.

However, both the rival extremes of behaviorism and dualism characterize the issue in a way that presents false alternatives. The real problem lies in the faulty philosophical psychology animated by a desire to discover an "objective" standpoint. That is to say, both views see the distinctiveness of human action as being essentially unrelated to the perspective of the agent performing the action.

Unfortunately the objective "scientific" model has been increasingly predominant in the modern world, and as Barry Schwartz has suggested, it has had a decisive impact on contemporary understandings of what it means to be a person and thus how people order their lives. Our everyday conception of human nature is coming to approximate the "scientific" one. As Schwartz sees it, the "scientific" model is buttressed by a convergence of views.

> The "human sciences"—economics, sociology, anthropology, and psychology—are attempting to show that no aspect of human life can resist the power of scientific scrutiny.[11]

In particular, Schwartz thinks the methodologies of economics, evolutionary biology/sociobiology, and behaviorism are converging to produce a picture of an ahistorical, amoral, scientific self. Schwartz suggests that whatever happens in philosophical debate, these "scientific" views—which exclude moral questions as irrelevant and deem intention and purpose as unnecessary to an adequate depiction of action—are winning "the battle for human nature" and are increasingly determining how human life is ordered.

Despite the influence of these views, they fail to capture the meaning and significance of human action as well as what it means to be a person. Clifford Geertz has aptly described the behaviorist image of "rational economic man" as "the moral equivalent of fast food, not so much artlessly neutral as skillfully impoverished."[12] But in order to recognize it as impoverished the alternatives need to be kept alive. As Schwartz's argument aptly points out, the alternatives have to be established not only at the level of philosophical argument but also in everyday life.

Fortunately, however, there is an alternative to the behaviorist and the dualist views of human action, and to the philosophical psychology which underlies them. On this alternative view, the agent's perspective and action are essentially related. It abandons the scientific model of the self, and in its place attempts to understand human life in more "agential" terms.

1.12 An Agential Understanding of Human Action and Human Life

On an agential understanding, action is qualitatively different from non-action in that actions are, as Charles Taylor puts it, "intrinsically directed." Actions are in a sense inhabited by the purposes or intentions which direct them; hence "action and purpose are ontologically inseparable."[13] Intentions exist only in terms related to the action itself and vice-versa; they cannot be separated into a dualism, nor can intentions be ignored.

For something to be a human action as distinguished from a bodily movement, not only must the physical movement cohere with other descriptions by which actions of this kind are characterized, an agent's intention or purpose must be to achieve this result. To recognize the importance of intention is to show that to know *what* the action is, or even *that* it is an action, can only be determined with reference to an agent's intentions.

The primary way in which intention is linked to action is in terms of action description and the predication of responsibility. G. E. M. Anscombe argues that action X is an intentional action if the agent's answer to the question "Why are you X-ing?" gives a reason for acting.[14] What characterizes an action as intentional is the agent's understanding of what she is doing, that it is related to the accomplishing of some end or goal. Action is intentional in the sense that agents form the action in accordance with their own reasons and descriptions of the situation. Intention and action are thus dialectically related: an action has to be described as an enacted intention, and an intention as an implicit action.

Within this understanding of the relation between action and intention, any action will fall under different descriptions, not all of which will be intentional. For example, Alasdair MacIntyre notes that to the question "What is he doing?" the answer might be

"digging," "planting lettuce seedlings," "making sure that they will have an adequate source of vitamin C," "doing what his wife told him," "taking his prescribed twenty-minute exercise," "filling in time till the bars open," "earning money," "overstraining his heart," "using the wrong tool for the job."[15]

The correctness of any one of these descriptions is compatible with the correctness of any (or even all) of the other descriptions. Moreover, the description provided by the agent may vary depending on the context in which he is asked about what he is doing. Eric D'Arcy develops the point nicely in considering the case of a clerk who is diligently at work at his desk two hours after his office has officially closed for the evening:

To the question, 'What are you doing?', [the clerk] may give different answers to different inquiries. For instance, to his wife on the telephone he may say, 'I'm working late;' to the manager of the firm, 'I'm finishing the Blair contract at the request of the Department Head;' to the Department Head, 'I'm just beginning the last clause;' to the policeman who has noticed the light burning unusually late, 'It's quite all right, Officer, I work here;' to a trade union official, 'It's all right, I'm getting double rates for working overtime.' Each of these different answers may be perfectly true and, according to the particular concern of each questioner, perfectly appropriate.[16]

The possibility of different true descriptions of an action and the recognition that descriptions may vary depending on the interests of the inquirer and/or the narrator are important for how action is to be understood in relation to the agent who performs the action.

The recognition of the possibility of multiple descriptions of an action leads Alasdair MacIntyre to distinguish among primary, secondary, and tertiary descriptions of an action. A primary description specifies an agent's primary intention or intentions; a secondary description specifies those intentions which the agent formulated in order to implement his primary intentions; and a tertiary description is a non-intentional characterization of what the agent does.[17]

The fact that there are different levels of description does not, however, necessitate the conclusion that the agent herself is the final authority in determining which descriptions are primary rather than secondary. Other people may have a better perspective of what is going on than the agent does herself. The agent could be judged wrong in her descriptions, as arguments about self-deception illustrate.[18] All that is necessitated by the different levels is the conclusion that the agent's perspective is indispensable to the characterization of the action.

The distinction between action and non-action, then, is one that occurs to agents. As Taylor argues, "a basic, not further reducible distinction between action and what just happens is indispensable and ineradicable from our self-understanding as agents."[19] What separates action from non-action is not some kind of Humean "cause"; it is that humans have the capacity to act and to provide descriptions of that act. As Taylor suggested in his earlier work,

> To speak of an 'intentional description' of something is to speak not just of any description which this thing bears, but of the description which it bears for a certain person, the description under which it is subsumed by him. Now the notion of an action as directed behavior involves that of an intentional description.[20]

The capacity to act, the capacity to provide "intentional descriptions," is fundamental to the whole range of moral behavior and the activity of making moral judgments. Both behaviorism and dualism are unable to account for the ways in which people distinguish (for both moral and legal purposes) different types of murder, or even the conclusions people reach in determining that murder was or was not committed even when confronted with what (from an external point of view) may appear to be the "same" event. The conclusion reached, then, is that action and agency are internally related such that the agent's perspective is ineliminable.

This understanding of action presents an alternative that dissolves the dispute between behaviorists and dualists. Action cannot be understood through the notions of an undiscriminated event and a particular kind of Humean cause (whether determined physiologically, sociologically, or psychologically), for this is to explain the action in terms of other primitive concepts. It appears that action is itself a primitive concept.

I say *appears* because the version of the agent's perspective thus far presented is subject to a substantive critique. The core of the critique, advanced by Charles Landesman and Richard Bernstein (among others), is that such a view results in a "new dualism."[21] Different from the dualism of mind and body, this is a dualism of two different and logically incompatible conceptual languages: the language of action and reason explanations versus the language of movement and mechanical causal explanation. The dualism occurs, so Bernstein argues, because of the claim that action is itself a primitive concept.

> To say that the category of action or agency is basic to our conceptual framework is to say man is a being who really acts, really does things, is sometimes motivated by reasons and not by causes. But we hope to show that the apriorism implicit in conceptual analysis is just as unwarranted as the apriorism implicit in reductive analysis. . . . Pervading the claims and counterclaims concerning the reducibility or nonreducibility of the concept of action, there have been two false pictures that have been responsible for much of the polemic.[22]

The two false pictures present an unpalatable dichotomy: either reductive mechanism (behaviorism and dualism) or anthropomorphic subjectivism (the dependency of the agent's perspective).

The danger of this "new dualism" is evident in the early work of Stanley Hauerwas. His book *Character and the Christian Life* represents a significant attempt to rehabilitate the notion of character as central to depictions of the moral life. In so doing he provides an extended discussion of the nature of action and its relation to personal agency. While he clearly rejects behavioristic and dualistic understandings of the self, he at times lapses into the "new dualism."[23] Note the following passage:

> Much of men's behavior must be thought of in terms of action rather than movement, for movement may be purposive but it cannot be intentional. "Action is not teleological, but intentional. It is described and understood by reference to the purpose of the agent." This difference also shows why action is ultimately an agent-concept, since only the agent can supply the description of what the action was; whereas purpose can be characterized from the observer's point of view.[24]

While Hauerwas is right in his claim that the agent's perspective is ineliminable from a description of an action—or more precisely, from the concept of action as such—and that this perspective should even be granted a certain priority in that description, he still lands himself in a new kind of dualism. Hauerwas's argument does not represent a crude version of the new dualism, for he makes the distinction between agents and observers. However, Hauerwas's use of the category of "observer" is primarily a distinction between action and movement, and so he remains caught in the binds of dualism.

Given the danger of the new dualism, what is the next step? The position I have been developing is not incorrect, it is inadequate. To make the position adequate, I will need to revise the claim that action is a primitive concept, and also show how the agent's perspective is bound up with other persons' in such a way that the dichotomy between "agents" and "observers" is dissolved. The second step will be the focus of the next section, but the first step can be resolved relatively easily.

The difficulty with the claim that action is a primitive concept is that it seems to result in a dualism between action and other types of events, and that consequently decisions about what should be described as an action are made exclusively by the agent. But as Alasdair MacIntyre has recently shown, the difficulty arises in trying to make action the primary issue. It is not action that is primarily at stake over against other "events," it is *intelligible* human action.[25] MacIntyre argues that it is a mistake to think "atomistically" about human action, for actions find their intelligibility by being placed in larger wholes. Life is more than a series of discrete, unrelated actions; it has a unity. To show this unity requires that actions be placed in particular contexts. In MacIntyre's terms,

> We identify a particular action only by invoking two kinds of context, implicitly if not explicitly. We place the agent's intentions, I have suggested, in causal and temporal order with reference to their role in his or her history; and we also place them with reference to their role in the history of the setting or settings to which they belong. . . . Narrative history of a certain kind turns out to be the basic and essential genre for the characterization of human actions.[26]

Narrative is thus crucial to the depiction of actions, for it is the narrative contexts which give actions their intelligibility.

MacIntyre contends that it is necessary to distinguish between intelligible and unintelligible actions. Unintelligible actions are "failed candidates for the status of intelligible action"; to lump the two types together in a single class of actions and then to characterize action in terms of what items both sets have in common is to miss this basic distinction. It is also to neglect the central importance of intelligibility. As MacIntyre describes it,

> To identify an occurrence as an action is in the paradigmatic instances to identify it under a type of description

which enables us to see that occurrence as flowing intelligibly from a human agent's intentions, motives, passions and purposes. It is therefore to understand an action as something for which someone is accountable, about which it is always appropriate to ask the agent for an intelligible account.[27]

Through the telling of narratives the agent is able to give an intelligible account of her actions.

Hence narrative is the crucial form for understanding human action. MacIntyre goes so far as to claim that human action in general is best understood as an "enacted narrative."[28] His conclusion is worth quoting at some length:

We always move towards placing a particular episode in the context of a set of narrative histories, histories both of the individuals concerned and of the settings in which they act and suffer. It is now becoming clear that we render the actions of others intelligible in this way because action itself has a basically historical character. It is because we all live out narratives in our lives and because we understand our own lives in terms of the narratives that we live out that the form of narrative is appropriate for understanding the actions of others.[29]

The importance of MacIntyre's analysis is that he places action not primarily at the level of *a priori* conceptual analysis, but rather in what Wittgenstein calls the "bustle of life."

Hence if intelligible action is more primitive than action *qua* action, and if action is made intelligible by placing it in narratives, then it appears that human life is best conceived in a narrative mode as well. Indeed MacIntyre argues that because narrative and action are mutually coimplicate, "man is in his actions and practice, as well as in his fictions, essentially a story-telling animal."[30]

But what does it mean to claim that human life is best conceived in terms of narrative? Four aspects of a narrative conception of human life need to be identified: (1) the narrative I live and tell is bound up with the narratives of other people, and those narratives are lived and told in particular social settings; (2) the unity of human life is the unity embodied in the narrative of a single life; (3) a narrative understanding allows no sharp distinction between reason and the passions/affections; and (4) the recognition that intentional action and subjection to various circumstances of human life are closely interrelated.

The narrative I live and tell is bound up with the narratives of other people, and those narratives are lived and told in particular social settings. There is, to be sure, a particularity to my narrative. As MacIntyre describes it, "I am what I may justifiably be taken by others to be in the course of living out a story that runs from my birth to my death; I am the *subject* of a history that is my own and no one else's, that has its own peculiar meaning." To be the subject of a narrative is thus "to be accountable for the actions and experiences which compose a narratable life."[31]

Such a claim about accountability "de-centers" the self by locating the particularity of my narrative in a complex set of interrelations with the narratives of other people's lives. In MacIntyre's words,

> I am not only accountable, I am one who can always ask others for an account, who can put others to the question. I am part of their story, as they are part of mine. The narrative of any one life is part of an interlocking set of narratives. Moreover this asking for and giving of accounts itself plays an important part in constituting narratives.[32]

Thus we are never more (and sometimes less) than the co-authors of our own narratives. We live life under certain constraints. "We enter upon a stage which we did not design and we find ourselves part of an action that was not of our own making. Each of us being a main character in his own drama plays subordinate parts in the dramas of others, and each drama constrains the others."[33] Cast in theological terms, the point needs to be made slightly differently. We are all participants in God's drama which constrains our own. Thus the interlocking narratives of human lives need to be understood within the larger context of our relation to the narrative of the Triune God.

Such a claim about the ways that the narratives of our lives are interlocked helps to explain why the description of an action is never wholly the property of the agent or of the observer. Indeed the character of interlocking narratives minimizes the significance of the very distinction between agents and observers. Learning to describe our actions is one dimension of learning to describe our lives, and we do both through conversations and arguments (i.e., asking for and giving accounts of our narratives) with those around us.[34]

The second aspect of a narrative conception of human life is that the unity of human life, that which overcomes chaos and fragmentation amidst a person's many roles, duties, and activities, is the unity of a narrative embodied in a single life. Of course there is no one way of characterizing such unity, and such unity as there is always lies on the other side of complexity.[35]

MacIntyre argues that the lived narrative which eventually provides unity to human life is characterized by unpredictability and teleology. The narrative of human life is unpredictable in that while there are constraints on how the narrative can continue, within those constraints there are indefinitely many ways it can continue.[36] The narrative of human life has a teleological character in that there "is no present which is not informed by some image of some future and an image of the future which always presents itself in the form of a *telos*—or a variety of ends or goals—towards which we are either moving or failing to move in the present."[37]

In light of both unpredictability and teleology, MacIntyre argues that the unity of human life is the unity of a narrative quest. Such a quest cannot even begin unless there is at least a partly determinate conception of the final *telos*. At the same time, however, the quest is also unpredictable in that the *telos* is never wholly adequately characterized. So MacIntyre concludes that a quest "is always an education both as to the character of that which is sought and in self-knowledge."[38]

Three important implications follow from this argument. The first is that while on this view the quest is undertaken from within a determinate social context—allowing for a diversity of quests—the view is not necessarily linked either to a relativism or a rabid historicism. Despite MacIntyre's rather unfortunate overstatement that "the good life for man is the life spent in seeking for the good life for man,"[39] a partly determinate conception of the *telos* is predicated on a realist conception of the good. A focus on MacIntyre's seemingly circular statement, along with his rejection of Aristotle's "metaphysical biology," has led some to charge him with voluntarism or relativism.[40] Precisely what MacIntyre means by a "partly determinate" *telos* remains ambiguous. Nonetheless, I think MacIntyre does want—or at least he should want—to preserve a certain "natural" teleology by maintaining a realistic objectivity about the good.[41] Thus the first implication is the claim that there is an objective *telos*, even if people are never able to grasp it wholly adequately, toward which human life is to move and in which humans will find the virtues perfected and/or fulfilled.[42]

A second implication follows closely on the first. If there is such a *telos* it by no means requires the view that only one way of configuring the virtues, or of construing human life, can be normatively recommended. A plurality of models of character can be all compatible with the attainment of the *telos*.[43] The only criterion (at least on the theological conception I will be developing) is that these multiple models, though not necessarily compatible contingently, need ultimately to complement each other. The corollary to such a view is that there must be a harmony, but not necessarily a unity, of the virtues.[44]

The third implication, one which both builds on and deviates from MacIntyre's argument, is that this unity by no means entails a linear conception of the narrative. There will undoubtedly be some dramatic reversals, false starts, wrong turns, and the like. Hence there is a difference between "constructive" narration and "reconstructive" narration.[45] Constructive narration is what a person is involved in as she lives into the future; she is constructing her narrative, involved in the quest of moving toward her *telos*. Reconstructive narration occurs when she retrospectively judges her actions and her life in an attempt to unmask her deceptions and make her narrative more truthful. Because self-deception has such a powerful hold on people's lives, reconstructive narration requires the presence of other persons, texts, and (Christians will argue) God to challenge the agent to tell the narrative of her life less untruthfully.[46] The narrative unity of human life involves both prospective orientation (toward the *telos*) and, more determinatively, retrospective judgment (reconstructing the narrative).

The third aspect of the narrative view of human life is that there can be no sharp separation between reason and the passions/affections. The grounds for separating them are either a false elevation of rationality as that which distinguishes humans from other creatures or a false denigration of the passions as animal intrusions awaiting reason's control. There is a rationality to the

emotions and an emotional quality to reason that is ne-
glected only at our peril. While disruptive passions do
need to be disciplined, affective feelings need to be cul-
tivated for wise moral judgment. Put succinctly, both
reason and affection are essential for the development
in, and activity of, virtuous living.

The fourth aspect of a narrative view of human life is
that it brings into much closer relation the capacity for
intentional action and our subjection to various circumstances of human life. There is a close relationship between being *a* subject and being subject. Richard Bondi
has identified three different ways in which persons are
subjected to what he calls "the accidents of history": (1)
events which are beyond the control of any individual
or group, (2) circumstances in which people simply find
themselves, and (3) the past, insofar as people cannot
change what has already occurred.[47] In more explicitly
political terms, the work of Michel Foucault has shown
the impact of various ways in which people are subjected to regimes of power and knowledge.[48] This close
relationship between being *a* subject and being subject
is reflected both in the capacity for understanding human lives in narrative terms and in the reversals and
disruptions which characterize those narratives.

A narrative conception of human life calls attention
to the particular contexts in which people find themselves, contexts in which people act and suffer. Indeed
human acting and suffering, and the descriptions of
those actions and that suffering, are closely tied to their
social contexts and the traditions of which they are a
part. It is important to learn to describe and redescribe
situations truthfully, for those descriptions and rede-
scriptions affect the sorts of activities in which people
engage. Indeed people's situations are inescapably linguistic. As I will show in the next section, learning how
to describe and redescribe occurs through social contexts, relationships, and practices.

1.2 THE SOCIAL CONTEXT OF MORAL DESCRIPTION

Through language people learn how to act and to feel, how to describe what they think and what they do. A person does not know how to characterize an action as this or that apart from the linguistic resources the agent draws from her social contexts. This was one of the fundamental points Wittgenstein made in his philosophy of language. As Fergus Kerr describes Wittgenstein's argument,

> Perhaps it is only if we are already strongly tempted to treat the self as a solitary intellect locked within a space that is inaccessible to anyone else that language looks intuitively like a system of referring to things.[49]

Wittgenstein's project is to undermine the view of human life which separates people's agency from the language they use.

For example, on the very first page of the *Philosophical Investigations* Wittgenstein moves meanings out of the infant Augustine's head to retrieve them in the mundane transactions of a village store. After quoting Augustine on naming, Wittgenstein shows how naming is inextricably intertwined with other activities:

> Now think of the following use of language: I send someone shopping. I give him a slip marked "five red apples". He takes the slip to the shopkeeper, who opens the drawer marked "apples"; then he looks up the word "red" in a table and finds a colour sample opposite it; then he says the series of cardinal numbers—I assume that he knows them by heart—up to the word "five" and for each number he takes an apple of the same colour as the sample out of the drawer.—It is in this and similar ways that one operates with words.[50]

Although Wittgenstein exaggerates the activity of the shopkeeper to make his point, he shows that the activity of linking objects with words presupposes the ability to do a good deal else. That is to say, the point of language does not lie in human minds, but in what people do together.

At this point the connection between my earlier discussion of action and this account of language becomes clear. Wittgenstein's claim about language is similar to MacIntyre's argument that intelligible action is more primitive than action as such. Wittgenstein continues the story of the shopkeeper by asking:

> —"But how does [the shopkeeper] know where and how he is to look up the word 'red' and what he is to do with the word 'five'?"—Well, I assume that he *acts* as I have described. Explanations come to an end somewhere.—But what is the meaning of the word "five"?— No such thing was in question here, only how the word "five" is used.

Wittgenstein's point seems to be that the scene in the shop is itself an intelligible instance of human behavior. There is no need to postulate some more primitive action. In fact, Kerr may be right in commenting that Wittgenstein drags out the shopkeeper's actions precisely to mock the idea that he needs to behave "consciously" as the dualist picture asserts.[51]

What is important to grasp from Wittgenstein's illustration is that human language and human action are inextricably tied to shared human activities. In Kerr's words, "The 'essence' of human language is the round of collaborative activity that generates the human way of life."[52] Language is an activity that proceeds not by monologue but through conversation and argument.

V. N. Voloshinov makes a similar point in his *Marx-*

ism and the Philosophy of Language.[53] Voloshinov rejects "objectivist" and "subjectivist" accounts of language, insisting that language is tied to dialogical social contexts. As he puts it,

> The actual reality of language-speech is not the abstract system of linguistic forms, not the isolated monologic utterance, and not the psychophysiological act of its implementation, but the social event of verbal interaction implemented in an utterance or utterances.[54]

In ways that are strikingly similar to Wittgenstein, Voloshinov elsewhere argues that meaning is tied to context and that the utterance is a social phenomenon.[55] Dialogue and a focus on social contexts are thus crucial to understanding language.

Earlier I utilized MacIntyre's and D'Arcy's explanations of how there can be multiple true descriptions of an action to show the importance of the agent's perspective. But those explanations more precisely reveal that there is no irreducible priority to the "agent's perspective," for conversations and arguments in particular social contexts are equally fundamental to the tasks of description and evaluation. A person does not give reasons for her action-descriptions for every act that she performs; to do so would be impossible. A person is in action constantly, and only occasionally does she stop to provide descriptions of those actions. Most of human action is a learned, habitual, and often unreflective reaction to the manifold pressures and dimensions of the social contexts in which a person acts. But that is not to say that such action is thereby unintelligible. An action is rendered intelligible by being located in specific kinds of social contexts; hence precisely because it is routine the action is *prima facie* intelligible.

When a person does provide descriptions, it is generally because she is asked to do so; in other words, descriptions arise in the context of a social exchange, a conversation or an argument. A person gives descriptions of her actions in response to inquiries or challenges.[56] Because it is possible to imagine a variety of contexts in which inquiries or challenges are made, there are multiple true descriptions of any given event. The point of D'Arcy's example quoted above is that "the description of an act appropriate to a given occasion may vary with the specialized interest of the inquirer or narrator."[57] There is no question about what is physically occurring: the clerk is moving his pencil with his right hand while sitting in a chair behind a desk.[58] What is being requested by each person is to make that physical behavior intelligible in terms the inquirer can understand. In D'Arcy's terms, the question is what *interest* the inquirers have in the situation. Their interest is aroused because the clerk's activity has something to do with a matter of *significance* to them (e.g., the wife is preparing dinner, the manager is closing the office).

Thus social contexts are fundamental to the descriptions of actions. Through conversations and arguments people ask for and are able to ascertain the intelligibility of actions otherwise in doubt. The problem is not simply how to characterize action *qua* action as distinguished from a mere bodily movement by an individual; the problem is how to give our actions intelligibility in response to the inquiries and challenges of other persons (or, in a different way, inquiries and challenges of ourselves).

Persons are agents in practical intercourse with one another, not solitary observers gazing outward (as in behaviorism) nor inward (as in dualism). A human being is constituted by shared languages and social contexts, the regular and patterned reactions persons have to one another. Human life is founded in dealings with one another—in actions and reactions, in what people do and what they suffer. Kerr's comment is an instructive summary: "Community is built into human action from the beginning."[59]

Thus it is in and through specific social contexts that actions are given intelligibility, that people learn not only the routinized and habitual forms of activity but also an understanding of how the possible descriptions of various actions should be ordered. Much of what is at stake in the activity of moral judgment is the degree to which agents are able intelligibly to describe and evaluate the situation and the actions involved.

When people ask and are asked for descriptions of actions, it is often because a moral matter is at stake. By moral I mean something similar to Stuart Hampshire's suggestion:

> One of the few universally accepted connotations of the word 'moral' is 'important': no moral question can also be trivial, and not worth careful consideration. A man's morality is shown by the type of questions of conduct that he takes seriously, by the type of decisions about which he is prepared to reflect carefully, and to entertain genuine and reasoned regrets and criticisms.[60]

By "important" Hampshire does not necessarily mean monumental, or even of great consequence; he does not exclude the routine and the mundane. What Hampshire does claim is that people, both as individuals and as social groupings, pick out some descriptions as important in ways they do not pick out others. Morality is something which is "out there," but it is not limited to that.

In *Moral Notions*,[61] Julius Kovesi attempts to dissolve the so-called "fact-value" distinction by showing how language shapes not only values but also the reading of the so-called "facts." He also shows how crucial social contexts are to the formation of moral judgments without lapsing into either relativism or subjectivism. Kovesi's argument is rather difficult to follow, so it will be necessary to take a rather circuitous route in order to understand the significance of his claims.

Kovesi thinks that moral notions have been wrongly understood as strictly "valuing" notions, and that the distinctions between moral and nonmoral notions have consequently been wrongly made. Contemporary moral thinkers often suggest that moral notions are different from notions about the physical world because the former "evaluate" reality while the latter "describe" it. Thus there is assumed to be a crucial difference between the moral notion of "murder" and the scientific notion of "table" or "coffeepot." But Kovesi thinks moral notions like "murder" are far more like notions such as "table" or "coffeepot" than unlike them.[62] Hence Kovesi begins his analysis with a discussion of "tables" before discussing "murder" and finally morality as a whole.

Kovesi suggests that both the empirical characteristics of an object or action and its function figure into our subsuming it under some notion (e.g., "table") or giving it a description (e.g., "that is a table"). In order conceptually to distinguish these features, Kovesi refers to the empirical characteristics as the "material" elements, and the function as the "formal" elements. So, for example, the material elements of a notion "table" include the great variety of physical materials and designs by which a table can be made. The formal elements of the notion "table" answers the question, What purposes do tables serve?

Likewise, there are a variety of ways of illegitimately killing someone (the material element of the notion of murder) but only when people have grasped the point of or reason for murder (the formal element) are people able to recognize a particular instance of murder and call it by the right name.[63] The material and formal elements are interrelated, of course, but Kovesi stresses the priority of the formal element:

Without [it] there is just no sense in selecting, out of many others, those features of a thing or an act that constitute it as that thing or act. Not only is there no sense in selecting those features, but some of those features simply would not exist at all, e.g. in the case of inadvertent acts there just would not be a by-product of an act [without a formal element having as its point 'inadvertence']. That without the formal element we cannot see the sense of selecting the material elements is especially important in connection with our moral notions. For the contemporary distinction between 'evaluation' and 'description' sometimes assumes that facts just *are* outside in the world waiting for us to recognize them; and that evaluation consists in selecting some facts on 'purely factual grounds' and then expressing our attitudes toward them, or making a decision about them.[64]

Thus what distinguishes moral notions from other notions is not that the former are "evaluative" while the latter are "descriptive," rather their formal elements are different. Moral notions are about reality as they pertain to people in a particular way.

Kovesi's central point can be put with reference to the particular interests and purposes of social groups. People use notions—moral and otherwise—to describe (i.e., arrange, construe) the world and human actions according to patterns which are meaningful to them as far as they are creatures who interact with the empirical world and who need and want to use it in certain ways rather than others. "In the case of our moral and social life . . . it is our wants and needs, aspirations and ideals, interests, likes, and dislikes that provide the very material for the formation of our notions."[65]

But Kovesi does not thereby draw the conclusion that it is possible to describe the world in just any way people choose. First, he insists on the point (drawn from Wittgenstein) that language is public. Words and notions exist in social groupings where they are shared. Societies share not only words but also reasons for selecting one notion rather than another in referring to objects and actions. Thus Kovesi insists that reasons "must be publicly testable and acceptable by anyone. Otherwise, people could not use the word in the same way, the word could not become part of our language."[66]

Second, people are not free to describe the world in just any way because a particular use of language places certain specifiable restraints upon the language-users (even if they may not know *a priori* how to apply these restraints to persons who do not share the same language, they cannot violate them with impunity).[67] For example, the description "coffeepot" is in an important sense *logically irrevocable.* Insofar as I am a participant in a coffee-drinking society which, because of its taste for hot coffee, its desire to brew it, and its need to pour it, has designated certain pieces of equipment as coffee-pots, then I am bound to that description. In Kovesi's language, this is "operating under a certain description." What this means is that it is not legitimate to give a description to one object, "this is a table," and withhold it from an identical object. Moreover, any change in our descriptions must be due to *relevant* factors. Pinches summarizes the point well:

> That is, there is a logic to any society's description which is based on the connection it has made in its notions between a given term and the empirical world— as we have explored in our discussion of recognitors. We cannot, for instance, hold up two objects which are identical except one is red and the other green and claim one is a coffeepot while the other is not. Color has nothing to do with being or not being a coffeepot—it is not a relevant difference; being red is not a recognitor of the notion of coffeepot.[68]

Hence descriptions do not, and cannot, change simply as individuals see fit; language is public, and particular descriptions (once located in a linguistic community) in important ways are binding on the language-users.

A social group's notions are not simply constructs which can be manipulated according to whim. They are, in a sense, a world themselves; and, as Pinches notes, this world "encroaches on the empirical world insofar as it imports its own relations and designates significance."[69] Kovesi makes the point as follows:

> In an important sense, in the [empirical] world there *is* no value and there are no murders, tables, houses, accidents or inadvertent acts. But our language is not about *that* world in which there is no value or no tables, houses, accidents or inadvertent acts. That world, the world of raw data, cannot be described for the sense of that world also lies outside it and the very description of it, likewise, lies outside it.[70]

Kovesi may put the point too strongly (even though his first phrase qualifies the claim), for it is quite possible to argue that a tradition's descriptions can be claims of what the world in fact is—even though it must be admitted that they are claims which currently are falsifiable and thus must be only candidates for truth alongside other claims and descriptions. Nonetheless, Kovesi's primary point is worth underscoring: to be a language user, to have a history that shapes uses of language, is to accept descriptions and thereby to recognize that there are reasons for those descriptions and the values and purposes behind them.

It is important to note how this applies to a moral notion such as "murder." It is inappropriate to conclude that "murder is wrong" (which is, in a sense, a redundancy—once we know the concept of "murder" we also know that it is wrong) is true only in this society and not in another. What can be said, as Pinches notes, is that "'murder is wrong' is true insofar as 'murder' (or an equivalent in another language) designates certain actions as immoral."[71] As Kovesi puts it in a more recent essay,

> The reasons why we select certain features of our lives, actions and situations into one notion and describe them by one term is because certain configurations have moral significance. Taking away that reason is like taking away a king pin, and the whole configuration will fall apart and the bits and pieces will take their place in other, not necessarily moral, configurations, or just remain as scattered configurations, or just remain as scattered pointless pieces. And those features of our lives that are features because of their moral significance will cease to be features at all.[72]

The consequence of accepting, at least in broad outline, the tenets of Kovesi's project is not simple fideism or moral relativism; it can still be claimed that actions designated by one tradition as "murder" are immoral regardless of who performs them. But what must be recognized is that descriptions are inextricably tied to the resources and practices of linguistic communities.

This points to a third reason descriptions cannot be changed according to whim, a reason that goes beyond and perhaps diverges from Kovesi's own views. A person does not simply risk inconsistency in once designating an object "table" and later revoking that description. People do not simply "reinvent the wheel" in each generation by deciding on specific descriptions; rather notions are received historically and within socially embodied traditions which are the bearers of linguistic resources and judgments that have been developed over time and which give meaning to moral notions.

While people are restrained in their use of descriptions by public language and the historical developments of those descriptions within a tradition, they also are free to argue *within* that tradition that a notion should be redescribed. This is particularly apparent as traditions are faced with new situations (e.g., should a nuclear missile be called a "weapon"?). Moreover, it is what happens when scientists make new discoveries (e.g., note the developments in a notion like "gold"). But it is also possible to propose that other, ordinary notions like "coffeepot" should be changed. Pinches describes it as follows:

> This is not to rage against the existence or correctness of the notion of coffeepot, a fruitless enterprise, but it is to give reasons, perhaps transferred from other notions, as to why the reasons we came up with coffeepots in the first place are outweighed. For example, someone might argue that we don't need to pour coffee into cups—it tastes better when drunk straight from the container in which it is brewed. This, interestingly, is to argue historically—with a tradition and under a notion. It is not to step outside the notion.[73]

Even though it is essential to recognize that people are bound by notions because they are not private but public and because they are received historically, it is also possible (and often essential) to take issue with them.

Voloshinov points to an even more important reason that issue may need to be taken with received notions. Because language is tied to social contexts, and because those social contexts are tied to changing historical and economic conditions, language proceeds dialectically in relation to those conditions. As he puts it:

> As the economic basis expands, it promotes an actual expansion in the scope of existence which is accessible, comprehensible, and vital to man. The prehistoric herdsman was virtually interested in nothing, and virtually nothing had any bearing on him. Man at the end of the epoch of capitalism is directly concerned about everything, his interests reaching the remotest corners of the earth and even the most distant stars. This expan-

sion of evaluative purview comes about dialectically. New aspects of existence, once they are drawn into the sphere of social interest, once they make contact with the human word and human emotion, do not coexist peacefully with other elements of existence previously drawn in, but engage them in a struggle, reevaluate them, and bring about a change in their position within the unity of the evaluative purview. This dialectical generative process is reflected in the generation of semantic properties in language.[74]

Hence moral notions need to be continually assessed and evaluated in relation to changing social contexts, and that assessment and evaluation is a dialectical process.

Indeed, that issue can be taken with received notions is *because* notions are public (and therefore reason-giving is encouraged) and historical (and therefore reference can be made to new situations or discoveries and compared to the past). Notions and descriptions, given as they are within socially embodied traditions, provide ways to criticize inadequate notions and to make present experience intelligible in the light of the past while also providing a way to suggest new patterns for construing the world and human actions.

Thus descriptions of actions, while multiple, are not infinitely "re-describable." Particular traditions have noticed certain aspects of actions which are more or less important in ordering common life. These have been encapsulated in particular descriptions. Thus people discover that they have *reasons* to describe actions in one way rather than another, to form and employ certain kinds of notions rather than others. Moreover, these reasons may differ depending on the specific contexts in which the questions are asked.

Kovesi's argument dissolves the fact-value distinction and in the process shows both why the agent's perspective is ineliminable and why a dichotomy between agents and observers is unacceptable. An agent's descriptions of her actions, if they are to be intelligible, will be situated in the context of her beliefs—beliefs drawn from the social contexts in which she lives and the traditions of which she is a part. If descriptions of an action arise out of conversation, then the tie between action and particular social contexts is inescapable.

I have argued that moral judgment is an activity in which the depiction of actions cannot be separated from the character and intentions of the agent, and that both actions and agents are best understood in narrative terms. Moreover, I have suggested that the tasks of describing actions, the world, and human life are inextricably tied to social contexts and socially embodied traditions. But these sets of claims are interrelated in ways that have as yet not been adequately shown.

The interrelationships can be seen by way of a brief explication of Alasdair MacIntyre's conception of practices. MacIntyre defines a practice as follows:

> By a 'practice' I am going to mean any coherent and complex form of socially established cooperative human activity through which goods internal to that form of activity are realized in the course of trying to achieve those standards of excellence which are appropriate to, and partially definitive of, that form of activity, with the result that human powers to achieve excellence, and human conceptions of the ends and goods involved, are systematically extended.[75]

On MacIntyre's account, practical reasoning is an activity that is learned in and through practices. As he puts it, "we are only able to know ourselves from within as rational agents because and insofar as we can be known by others as rational agents in virtue of our participation with them in practices."[76]

This suggests that moral judgment is an activity that

is learned and exercised in and through shared practices. But the issues are actually more complex than that. Many moral judgments are made and actions performed as part of the everyday routines of persons in their social contexts. When there is doubt about why an action has been performed and/or a judgment made, practices take on a focal role because it is in the conversation and/or argument which emerges in and through practices that actions are made intelligible and judgments are justified. But it is also the case that a particular person's narrative has a crucial role to play in the reasons given for the action performed or judgment made. Hence as MacIntyre observes,

> Actions can be intelligible or unintelligible in at least three different ways: in the ways they conform to or in the ways that they depart from the standards provided by the structures of everyday routines, in the ways that they conform to or depart from the standards of practices and in the ways that they conform to or depart from the standards embodied in narratives; but their intelligibility or unintelligibility does not arise from the simple facts of conformity or departure, but from the reasons which the agent has (or fails to have) for such conformity or departure.[77]

In each case, a person's particular descriptions of her reasons for acting are shaped by her tradition's stock of descriptions, a stock limited by the contemporary condition of practices and the availability of narrative forms. Practices thus are central for the activity of moral judgment and the description of actions, the world, and human life. As MacIntyre puts it,

> The general form of the thesis which I have defended is that genuinely human consciousness is such that our abilities to reflect upon and thus to be knowledgeably conscious of our inner lives—insofar as those inner lives

are a matter of intending, doing, having reasons for
action and believing—depends upon our abilities to interact socially with others within practices and to understand what they impute to us. We learn to recognize
what is true about ourselves in this area and we learn
to describe ourselves only as others recognize and describe us and we learn to recognize and describe those
others precisely as beings capable of recognizing and
describing us in the way that they do.[78]

MacIntyre thus shows how the activity of relating
agents to the actions they perform, rendering each intelligible through narrative construals, is inextricably tied
to shared practices in which people learn to describe
themselves and their actions in one way rather than
another.

MacIntyre's conception of a practice is, at least in
some respects, quite close to Kovesi's characterization
that social groups have particular interests and purposes for describing things in one way rather than another. But whereas Kovesi's appeals to *anyone* lend an
abstractness to his analysis, MacIntyre specifies how
practices and narratives are tied to accounts of moral
traditions. In developing what he calls the "core concept" of virtue, MacIntyre develops three stages in the
logical development of the concept:

> The first stage requires a background account of what I
> shall call a practice, the second an account of what I
> have already characterized as the narrative order of a
> single human life and the third an account a good deal
> fuller than I have given up to now of what constitutes
> a moral tradition. Each later stage presupposes the ear-
> lier, but not *vice versa*.[79]

Kovesi's analysis is helpful in explicating the first component in MacIntyre's proposal, how the description of
moral notions is related to particular practices. My ac-

count of the importance of narrative for construing action, agency, and their interrelation is important for understanding the second component's relation to moral judgment. But a more complete account of the relationship of traditions to moral judgment is needed.

1.3 MORAL DESCRIPTION, MORAL JUDGMENT, AND THE PLACE OF TRADITIONS

MacIntyre's argument about practices specifies in a way in which Kovesi's argument does not the important role socially embodied traditions play in the activities of moral description and hence also moral judgment. Traditions are the carriers of specific moral notions, judgments that, for example, this is murder and that "killing in self-defense," or that, as the Aristotelian tradition affirms but the Christian tradition denies, magnanimity is a virtue and humility is a vice. Those notions are tied to theological (or antitheological or atheological) judgments, as can be seen by a brief discussion of how the language of "suicide" has been employed in two quite diverse social contexts, twelfth- and twentieth-century Japan.

In a recent essay Alasdair MacIntyre has argued against positivist sociology (as represented by Durkheim) that there is no single phenomenon "suicide" that can be applied to any and all situations and social contexts. According to MacIntyre, "The intention embodied in suicidal acts must always presuppose some more or less determinate conception of what it is to die and what it is to bring about someone's death. As such conceptions vary, so will the phenomenon of suicide."[80]

MacIntyre rightly shows how in diverse social contexts the taking of one's own life can have quite different meanings and be subjected to quite different evaluations. He contrasts the self-inflicted death of Minamoto no Yoshitsune in twelfth-century Japan, performed to preserve his honor in the face of imminent defeat and done in accordance with Buddhist Scriptures, with a modern Japanese person who takes his own life because he is unable to cope with the burdens of trying to succeed. MacIntyre draws the conclusion that the two deaths, and hence the evaluation of the two acts, are quite different: different on the one hand because the former is a reflection of triumph over imminent defeat while the latter is a reflection of total defeat, different on the other hand because the former is an act which can express the achievement of a supreme good while the latter expresses the frustration of the individual's practical reasoning by external social circumstance.[81]

But while MacIntyre nicely indicates how the notion of suicide is bound up with broader conceptions of what it means to live and to die and/or to bring about someone's death, he is inadequately attentive to whether the language of "suicide" ought to be applied in both social contexts. MacIntyre refers to Yoshitsune's act of taking his own life as a "ritual suicide." But it is not clear that a traditional Japanese conception of *hara kiri*, in which the act of willfully taking one's own life is bound up with conceptions of honor, is morally equivalent to the notion of suicide. While Yoshitsune (and others in his culture) would acknowledge that he had taken his own life and that he had good reason to do so, he would not likely describe it as a justifiable exception to the generally assumed prohibition against suicide; rather he would see it as the positive expression of a commitment to which he was morally bound by honor. Cast in theological terms, the loss of the Buddhist context in the twentieth-century example significantly alters both the description and the judgment made about what might otherwise appear to be rather similar "events" (i.e., the taking of one's own life).

Why do I employ such a loaded term as "tradition"

to designate the context-dependent character of moral description and moral judgment? An answer requires a more careful delineation of what I mean by such a notion, and in part that will be accomplished by differentiating my conception from three alternative views.

My stake in what I identify as "traditions" is closely tied to my overall argument that theological (or antitheological or atheological) claims make a decisive difference for the moral life. Moral description and moral judgment (and thus moral education) are tied to particular social contexts; and those social contexts reflect and embody theological (or antitheological or atheological) views about such matters as God, the world, and life and death. An account of moral judgment is "traditioned" in the sense that there is no way to avoid taking a stance about such matters. To refuse to take a stance as a pragmatist such as Richard Rorty does is a way of taking a stance (albeit an atheological one) that includes some descriptions and excludes others.

My appeal to the notion of a tradition, then, does not imply a necessarily conservative stance toward a particular social order, as would be the case for a follower of Edmund Burke. The particular arguments and commitments of a tradition, and of the accounts of the virtues and moral judgment tied to that tradition, may be "revolutionary" or "radical" in terms of many social orders—as I would suggest a Christian account is likely to be.[82]

In *After Virtue* MacIntyre's argument stresses the importance of traditions, but his focus is on *socially embodied* traditions. His argument emphasizes the relationship between social contexts and moral claims. In *Whose Justice? Which Rationality?*[83] however, MacIntyre develops an argument about "traditions of enquiry" in which the tie between social contexts and moral claims is much looser (and sometimes absent from his explicit discussion). Thus his accounts of Aristotle, Augustine, and

Thomas (much less liberalism) and their respective "traditions" end up curiously abstracted from the social contexts which are so important for the intelligibility and justification of theological and moral claims.

My account of tradition is not connected to MacIntyre's latter sense of tradition, as on my view a "tradition of enquiry" ought to occur within the social contexts of particular patterns of friendships, practices, and beliefs. Too often such "traditions of enquiry" freewheel in abstraction from the particular social contexts in which people find themselves and from which they draw their descriptions. Indeed in *Whose Justice? Which Rationality?* MacIntyre tends toward providing a philosophical account of the history of ideas. Such a tendency is problematic in two interrelated ways. First, in making such a move MacIntyre fails to provide adequate attention to the ways we learn and fail to learn to make enquiries and judgments in and through particular social contexts.

Second, MacIntyre fails adequately to specify how divergent judgments about God, the world, and life and death among such figures as Aristotle, Augustine, Aquinas, and Hume both arise from different social contexts and lead to different descriptions of those social contexts and of the judgments people are called on to make. Because the ways in which people live and act and argue about how they should live and act invariably reflect judgments about theological matters, one cannot understand different moral traditions without appreciating the role of theological (or antitheological or atheological) views in those traditions. In short, MacIntyre does not adequately attend to the ways in which the arguments of Aristotle, Augustine, Aquinas, Hume, and various liberals are bound up with particular social and historical circumstances. He also does not adequately recognize that those arguments reflect at least partially competing theological (and antitheological and atheological) judgments. My disagreement with MacIntyre, however, occurs within a much larger agreement about moral description, moral judgment, and the importance of the virtues.

There is a second alternative view in which that larger agreement does not exist. This view entails the denial that traditions employ morally distinct "languages," the proponents of such a view claiming that the mere fact of a diversity of descriptions and traditions does not mean that traditions provide the central contexts for moral judgment.

Alan Donagan's complex attempt to unite a Kantian conception of rationality with appeals to the "Hebrew-Christian tradition" in order to provide *the* theory of morality is an example of such a view.[84] Donagan's proposal is an attempt to use reason to get at the tradition's philosophical essence such that the significance of tradition and the theological claims which accompany that tradition disappear. But Donagan's proposal stands firmly within a tradition that argues as if it is not a tradition and hence assumes a tradition is dispensable—namely, the Kantian tradition.[85]

What Donagan provides is a version of the "Hebrew-Christian tradition" which has Kant's theory of practical reason as a central component, and which is based on the contention that the theological commitments of the tradition are dispensable in providing a theory of morality. Donagan's account has at its center a Kantian "thin theory of the self" (autonomous, self-existent, end-in-itself) which he thinks can be used to explain away the divergences between the "Hebrew-Christian" tradition and (to take his example) the Hindu tradition. I have already given reasons why I think such an account of the self ought to be rejected, and why his attempt to factor out theological claims without loss is bound to fail. His very notion that there is a single "Hebrew-Christian" tradition reflects his failure to recognize the ways in which divergent theological claims also produce divergent moral judgments. His proposal does not succeed in avoiding theological claims or in providing an account which is not tradition-dependent.

There is a third alternative view that refuses the notion of tradition (and perhaps also moral judgment). The proponents of such a view contend that the notion of "tradition" presumes too much continuity and wrongly suggests a normative view. What is needed is not any kind of account of "tradition" but a Foucauldian genealogy which unmasks the pretensions to continuity and reveals the discontinuities and power-configurations which exist but are often concealed by such notions as traditions.

I think such a view ought to be rejected as an *alternative* to my account for three reasons. First, insofar as the genealogist *only* unmasks and is relentlessly critical, she thereby denies the possibility of *any* normative account whatsoever. Thus the accountability ingredient in *moral* judgment is rendered vacuous. Of course the genealogist could insist that there is no need for such a normative account.

Such a refusal is predicated on a mistaken philosophical psychology that fails to recognize how persons *learn* to feel, see, and act in one way rather than another. That is to say, even genealogists learn to provide the critical unmasking they think is necessary, but their argument does not include an account of how such learning takes place. This is the second reason for refusing this position as an alternative.

The third and closely related reason involves recognizing that the genealogist's position is tradition-dependent (in the sense I am using it) insofar as it entails specific theological (or antitheological or atheological) commitments. The genealogist, insofar as her work continues to be significantly indebted to Nietzsche, is typically antitheological (or perhaps by this point more likely atheological). The genealogical argument is thus not an alternative to my claim that theological (or antitheological or atheological) claims have a decisive impact on an account of the moral life; rather it offers a competing account based on divergent theological views.

That is *not* to say, however, that the substance of the genealogist's arguments should necessarily be rejected. In the second and third chapters I will offer an account that has been significantly influenced by the arguments of people like Foucault and Derrida. Walter Lowe has instructively shown some significant parallels between Derrida and Barth, and some of those same arguments are important to my account.[86] On the view I defend, what establishes the continuities of human identities and the continuities of traditions is the faithfulness of God, not anything ingredient in "selves" or "traditions." Thus there is no need for, or guarantee of, continuity in my account of tradition.

An account which is significantly influenced by genealogical criticism but is ultimately a theological account from within the Christian tradition is (at least partially) a different and divergent account from one that is genealogical and is ultimately nihilist. Both claims are tradition-dependent, but they are grounded in competing traditions which have different normative presumptions about how such matters as God, the world, and life and death should be understood.

Moral judgment, then, is an activity that is inextricably tied to theological (or antitheological or atheological) claims and commitments. Those claims and commitments arise out of, and are embodied in, various friendships and practices. Moreover, it is by being inducted into those friendships and practices that people learn to describe their actions, their lives, and the world in one way rather than another and are thus formed in moral judgment. As Jeffrey Stout suggests, "The only way to get people to enter [the logical space of moral judgment] is through successful moral training."[87]

Wittgenstein's description of how people gain sound judgment as to the genuineness of expressions of feeling is instructive on these matters.

> Can one learn this knowledge? Yes; some can. Not, however, by taking a course in it, but through 'experience.'—Can someone else be a man's teacher in this? Certainly. From time to time he gives him the right *tip*.—This is what 'learning' and 'teaching' are like here.—What one acquires is not a technique; one learns correct judgments. There are also rules, but they do not form a system, and only experienced people can apply them right. Unlike calculating rules.[88]

Put in the context of my argument, learning to make correct moral judgments involves learning particular modes of behavior. As Sabina Lovibond suggests,

> The use of moral concepts by individual speakers (as they progressively acquire competence in that area of language) is grounded in an increasingly diversified capacity for participation in social practices, i.e. practices mediated by language or other symbolic systems. But the induction of an individual into a communal form of life is a gradual process: until it is complete, there will be some 'correct judgements' which escape him, and hence some moral facts which transcend his awareness.[89]

This process of learning, involving the acquisition both of distinct modes of language and specific forms of behavior, is a life-long process. Again Lovibond's comments are instructive:

> As we make additions to our repertoire of 'correct judgements' in connection with a given moral concept, we acquire the *intuitive* basis for our next step up the

scale of forms of *reflective* specification of the content of that concept.[90]

Lovibond's views about language-acquisition and moral growth are rooted in the notion of "semantic depth," a concept borrowed from Mark Platts's *Ways of Meaning*.[91] Semantic depth suggests that a person can begin with a minimal and formal understanding of the "meaning" of a term or moral judgment, and then, through a progressive and more sustained engagement with the shared friendships and practices of the tradition which underlie those terms and judgments, she may deepen her understanding of the terms or judgments in question *without* necessarily coming to mean something different than was expressed earlier.

Hence an adequate account of the activity of moral judgment needs to attend not only to the formation *of* moral judgments but also to formation *in* moral judgment. The ways in which people describe their actions and their lives, and the ways in which people acquire and exercise the virtues necessary for wise moral judgment, are learned in and through particular friendships and practices.

Before turning to such friendships and practices from the standpoint of (a version of) the Christian tradition's depiction of God as Triune, however, I need to describe moral formation in more detail so as to guard against two possible misunderstandings. First, I need to show how and why the kind of moral formation that is necessary to moral judgment is not merely a non-rational process of childhood training, but is an ongoing process that occurs throughout life of habituation in modes of acting, feeling, and thinking well. Second, I need to show how and why such moral formation ought not to be simply a way of perpetuating ideologies through indoctrination, but involves ongoing practices of critical reflection.[92]

One of the sources for the view that moral training is basically a non-rational process of childhood training is an interpretation of Aristotle's comments at the end of Book I and the beginning of Book II of the *Nicomachean Ethics*. There he contends that moral virtue is acquired through the habituation of the non-rational part of the soul, in contrast to the excellence of the intellect which is acquired through teaching.[93]

But, as Nancy Sherman has instructively argued, this separation is at best provisional.[94] After adopting the Platonic division into rational and non-rational parts as "adequate enough" for his purposes at the time (*NE* 1102a26–28), Aristotle proceeds to qualify the distinction in chapter 13 of Book I until it almost disappears (see NE 1102b14, 1102b31). Moreover, in the *De Anima* Aristotle is even more resistant to dividing the soul into parts, contending that any divisions will always be relative to an inquiry and can be conceived and divided in different ways as well. In particular, he argues that the division in practical action is specious since the rational part must be seen as implying rational wish or desire.[95] Thus even on Aristotle's account, reason and desire are interrelated in ways which talk of separate parts of the soul fails to recognize.

Nancy Sherman, drawing on Aristotle's views, adopts the analogy of child and parent in order to show the relationship between reason and desire in both moral training and moral judgment. As she suggests, though a child's reason is guided externally by those older and wiser, they utilize the child's own perceptions, beliefs, and feelings to form her reasoning and foster understanding.[96] They teach the child to learn to deploy moral notions in describing particular situations, to learn how to identify the relevant features of the situation at hand. This involves using past experience and an imaginative and affective feel for how that experience is related to the particular situation facing her.

This process is itself a stage of reasoning, a process of discerning the particulars in a non-procedural way. It requires a grasp of the whole situation and an ability to describe the salient features in the appropriate manner and with finely discriminated linguistic skills. Moreover, it requires remaining close to the particular situation.[97]

Hence the person capable of making wise moral judgments will not only act well but also feel and think well. That is to say, proper virtuous choice requires both correct selection and correct emotional response. Thus moral formation is directed not only toward acting well but toward "being properly affected."[98] No matter whatever passions a person has by "nature," those passions can nonetheless be formed through moral training. "Although we may in some narrow sense not be responsible for our feelings, we are responsible for our character as the dispositional source of those feelings."[99]

Aristotle's main point about the interrelations of reason and the emotions is important to a Christian theological account.[100] The emotions are selective and responsive elements of human beings, and they play a crucial role in moral excellence. The emotions are thus educable; they have to be guided, made less blind, but nonetheless they are central to wise moral judgment.

Because the emotions are themselves a mode of discerning the particulars, the evaluative content of emotions cannot be solely cognitive. For example, to respond to a loved one who has just died is not typically to observe intellectually that she has died, and *then* feel grief; nor simply of knowing that she has died *because* one feels grief. It is rather seeing and discerning with a clarity and an intensity that is itself described by grief. The emotions themselves are modes of vision, and a deficiency in a person's emotions results in a deficiency in her capacity for moral judgment. As Nancy Sherman characterizes it, "Emotions shape and color how and what we see just as what we see refines and shapes how and what we feel. The capacities and functions are deeply intertwined."[101]

Hence the claim that moral formation is non-rational is at best misleading, at worst false. Reason and the emotions are inextricably interrelated, and moral formation ought to be directed toward both. It is inaccurate to see such formation as a mindless and/or passionless learning of a skill by merely doing right things so they become habitual. Rather, moral training is geared toward the formation of people who have appropriate thoughts and desires, and are thus disposed to judge wisely and to act well.

Such training in which people learn how to feel, to act, and to think also ought to include practices of critical reflective thought. Before indicating the place of such critical reflection, however, it is worth attending to the objection, one version of which has been advanced by Stanley Hauerwas in the "Introduction" to the third printing of his *Character and the Christian Life*, that the account of moral formation I am defending places too strong an emphasis on the rational dimension of character. He writes,

> I certainly do not mean to deny that people of character may possess extraordinary self-awareness. What I want to deny, however, is that such self-awareness is a necessary correlative to having character. For example, it may be quite sufficient for persons to claim their action as their own by saying simply "I am a Jew" or "I am a Christian". . . . The Mennonite farmer in central Indiana may be quite happy with his community and strikingly 'unaware' of himself, but that in no way disqualifies him from being a person of character. This example helps remind us that 'consciousness' is not a quality inherent to the individual, but rather is a skill made possible by our participation in a substantive community with an equally substantive history.[102]

There are some important ambiguities in Hauerwas's claim, such as what he means by claiming the Mennonite farmer as a "person of character." Insofar as he is claiming that an account of character is inextricably tied to socially embodied traditions, his point is well taken.

Hauerwas's point is also significant in its suggestion that rationality in Wittgenstein's sense of "knowing how to go on" does not require self-knowledge and self-awareness in the ways those notions are often understood. And, indeed, I am in sympathy with the claim that moral formation involves the kind of rationality of "knowing how to go on."

But there is a broader issue implicit in Hauerwas's claim: because accounts of character are tied to the narratives of socially embodied traditions, the carrier of rationality is the tradition such that the agent need not have either self-awareness or self-knowledge. Of course it is one thing to say that an action is *intelligible* by appealing to the narrative of a tradition, but it is quite another to attribute wisdom or character to the person who performs the action. As MacIntyre contends, "The educated moral agent must of course know what he is doing when he judges or acts virtuously. Thus he does what is virtuous *because* it is virtuous."[103] Hence the step going beyond making an action intelligible, namely attributing wisdom or character to the person who performed the action, typically requires knowledge.

Even more, Hauerwas's account underplays the significance of being able to think critically in new situations. As Agnes Heller puts it,

> [Repetitive thinking] can and very often does render us slow to recognize what is novel, and to identify the problems inherent therein. In problematic situations— i.e. in situations where inventive thinking is called for— we often try to get by or make do with repetitive thinking. As we shall see, this can lead to the catastrophes

of everyday life: more than this, it can also impede the development of the personality.[104]

The kind of inventive thinking Heller calls for is integral to what it means to be practically wise. It is learned in part through being trained to discern and respond to the particulars of new situations; and it is also learned through various practices of critical reflective thought ingredient in wise moral judgment.[105]

Because the goods of a tradition in general, and key moral and political notions in particular, are in part essentially contested, the kind of critical reflective thought signified by Heller's "inventive" thinking is important if the tradition is to grow and develop rather than stagnate or regress. Thus one reason practices of critical reflection are necessary is because neither friendships, practices (including the practices of critical reflection), nor traditions are static and immune to historical change and revision. As a consequence, people's connections to the friendships and practices of a tradition need to entail both commitment to those friendships and practices and reflective criticism of the ways in which they are deficient and distorted and/or can be improved and extended.

In this light, a second reason why critical reflective thought is necessary as a component of moral formation becomes apparent. Because of the ways in which friendships and practices can malform as well as form people, it is crucial that people are trained in practices of critical thought that enable them to recognize whether and under what conditions they would no longer be willing to participate in particular friendships and practices. The degree to which any specific friendships and practices need to be criticized is a *historical* question about the actual state of those friendships and practices and the health of that tradition. It requires what Clifford Geertz calls a "thick description" of the tradition and the social life that is the embodiment of the tradition.

Hence part of what is needed are practices of critical reflective thought similar to what Clodovis Boff calls "an ideo-political vigilance."[106] Such vigilance needs to be maintained toward the ways in which friendships, practices, and traditions can be distorted and corrupted. Such distortions and corruptions can occur for a variety of reasons: for example, institutional hegemony, cultural and economic influences, the lack of virtuous exemplars, abusive power and dominance, the influence of various distorting ideologies (all of which are themselves essentially contested notions). The goal of such critical thought, which occurs relative to particular contexts, is to repair as well as extend the particular friendships and practices of a tradition through which a person is formed and transformed in moral judgment.

While my account of the need for practices of critical reflective thought has perhaps emphasized the ways in which criticism of friendships and practices is necessary, there is no necessary presumption that criticism will always be the result. Indeed critical reflective thought may also lead to an endorsement of the friendships and practices under question. More likely, critical reflective thought will lead one both to endorsement and to criticism of the friendships and practices under consideration; which of the two ought to bear the greater weight cannot be decided in principle, for it can only be done with reference to specific cases and examples.

Thus the kind of account of moral formation I am defending ought to be neither a non-rational process of childhood training, nor a means of perpetuating ideologies through rigid indoctrination. It requires an ongoing process of helping people to learn to act, feel, and think well, and that process includes training in various practices of critical reflective thought. What is needed, then, is a more detailed account of how people acquire and exercise the virtues necessary for moral judgment in and through particular friendships and practices.

If my argument thus far is correct, however, then such an account needs to be developed from a particular standpoint. I have argued in this chapter (1) that moral judgment is inextricably tied to particular social contexts, (2) that moral descriptions are controversial and are hence tied to views about theological matters (such that there is no *one* specific Western history of morality nor any guaranteed presumption of "common ground" among diverse groups), and (3) that the activity of moral judgment requires moral education through induction into the friendships and practices of socially embodied and theologically specified traditions.

Thus my account needs to display the difference such a socially embodied and theologically specified tradition makes for an account of the moral life. I am convinced that the Christian depiction of God as Triune is central to the most coherent and truthful account of moral judgment and the moral life that can be offered. Thus in the next two chapters I will show how (at least one version of) the depiction of God as Triune provides the context for an account of specific kinds of friendships and specific kinds of practices ingredient in the moral education necessary for a person to become capable of making wise moral judgments.

2. LEARNING TO SEE AND ACT RIGHTLY

BECOMING PERSONS BY PARTICIPATING IN THE MYSTERY OF GOD

The activity of moral judgment is inextricably tied to particular social contexts and is decisively affected by the presence or absence of theological convictions of one sort or another. People *learn* to describe their actions and lives in one way rather than another, and people *learn* to acquire and exercise the virtues ingredient in making wise judgments. If moral judgment is an expression of the character of the person who offers it, and if depictions of character vary among socially embodied and theologically specified traditions, we need to inquire about how a person's character should be formed from the standpoint of a particular tradition.

My inquiries in this chapter and the chapter to follow are designed to show how and why the depiction of formation and transformation in moral judgment is integrally related to theological views. I will do so by providing an account of Christianity that connects belief in the Triune God to a distinctive shaping of the moral life and moral judgment. That distinctive shaping is also, I am convinced, the most truthful and coherent account of the moral life and moral judgment that can be offered. Defending that claim adequately, however, would require a different sort of argument, and a different sort of book, than I provide here.

On the account I offer, the shaping of the moral life is neither a linear and stable process of ongoing growth nor an oppositional dualism of before and after some dramatic turning point such as conversion. While I argue that the moral life should receive its decisive specification in the person and work of Jesus Christ, I also contend that it is a mistake to assume that this life should be exclusively understood as a matter of following Jesus. Instead I suggest that the moral life, understood most adequately in terms of Christian life, is to be lived in the mystery of the Triune God.

This chapter, which focuses on the relationship between the depiction of God as Triune and the task of becoming persons, moves through three sections. In the first section, I provide a brief discussion of friendships, practices, and the practices of friendship in order to set the context for my account of friendship with God and the friendships and practices of Christian life. In contrast to Alasdair MacIntyre's argument that practices are the means whereby the virtues are acquired, I suggest that both friendships and practices are necessary. What MacIntyre fails to recognize is that the virtues are dispositions of character; when attention is given to the formation of character, friendships become crucial for understanding the moral life. Hence it is important to understand the ways in which friendships and practices are interrelated in the moral life.

In the second and third sections of the chapter I argue that what really matters are not friendships and practices *per se*, but the friendships and practices which are intimately connected to living in the mystery of the Triune God. The second section sets the context for that account through a discussion of what it means to live in relation to such a God. The *telos* of Christian life is participation in the mystery that is the Triune God. That participation is made possible because of the history of God's love: the God who created humanity in God's image has once again enabled such participation by conforming humanity to Jesus Christ, the fulfillment of which lies in the consummation of God's Kingdom. On the view I develop, human life is ever precarious, marred both by the vicissitudes of history and struggles for identity. Thus it is a task to become that which for God people already are, namely citizens of God's Kingdom.

In the third section, I begin to spell out the shape of Christian life, the movement toward becoming the image of God. Although it is true that the practice of friendship is central to moral formation, Thomas Aquinas is accurate in claiming that the primary friendship people are called to have is with the Triune God. Humanity has been "befriended" by the Triune God through the person and work of Jesus Christ, and the proper response to being befriended is a life of transformative discipleship. Hence on this Christian account what is important is not only formation but *trans*formation in moral judgment. However, contrary to those accounts which stress conversion at the expense of formation, I argue that transformation and formation are inextricably interrelated. Finally, I argue that there is a plurality of ideals of discipleship, and that they find their completion only in and through the rich diversity which comprises Christian community.

2.1 FRIENDSHIPS, PRACTICES, AND THE PRACTICES OF FRIENDSHIP

If becoming a person requires being in relation to others, then a human being must *learn* to become a person by actively cultivating friendships and participating in practices that enable such relations to be developed and sustained. As people are formed in and through friendships with particular people and shared activities in particular practices, they are acquiring habits of acting, feeling, and thinking that are bound up with specific conceptions of the Good. Through particular kinds of friends, and paradigmatically through friendship with the Triune God, a person is inducted into the shared practices of Christian life. In so doing she is enabled to see the world, her life, and her actions in a distinctive and less untruthful way. She acquires the distinctive languages reflected in Christian practices, languages that are carried by the tradition and which serve to help constitute her identity.

In order to see how this is the case, it is necessary to attend more carefully to the relationship between friendships and practices. In contrast to Alasdair MacIntyre's account, I do not think that practices, even when seen in relation to the narrative unity of human life and when situated within traditions, provide the central means for acquiring the virtues.

Of course, MacIntyre's account is insightful. For example, MacIntyre claims that practices have two kinds of good: external and internal. External goods are those which can be achieved through the practice, but they are only contingently related to the practice. They can be acquired through other means. Goods internal to practices can only be specified by particular games or activities and by examples drawn from those games or activities; but more importantly, such internal goods "can only be identified and recognized by the experience of participating in the practice in question."[1]

Moreover, MacIntyre distinguishes practices from the institutions which are the bearers of the practices. Institutions, on his view, are necessarily and characteristically concerned with external goods (e.g., structured in terms of power and status, and are concerned with the acquisition and distribution of money, power, and status). But MacIntyre also rightly insists that no practices can survive for any length of time unsustained by institutions. While practices cannot do without institutions, they are also vulnerable to the acquisitiveness of the institution; in MacIntyre's words, "The cooperative care for common goods of the practice is always vulnerable to the competitiveness of the institution."[2] MacIntyre notes that though institutions have corrupting power if not checked by the exercise of the virtues, the making and sustaining of forms of human community—including institutions—have all the characteristics of a practice. Thus practices and institutions, though conceptually distinct and typically concerned with different kinds of good, are also closely related.

MacIntyre's account is flawed, however, because he attempts to make practices the primary context in which moral education occurs. He attempts to specify what he means by "practices" in a relatively technical and precise way, but he fails adequately to show the relationship between practices and the virtues.

For example, in a review essay of *After Virtue* Richard J. Bernstein argues that while a master chess player is one who knows how to take risks (i.e., exhibits courage) in chess, that person may lack this "virtue" for any other practice.[3] MacIntyre responds to the objection by arguing that "someone may of course use the type of behavior enjoined by a particular virtue skillfully to procure certain ends," and that Bernstein's objection fails because he does not distinguish between "the genuine exercise of a virtue and the behavior required by a virtue to achieve particular successes."[4]

Though Bernstein does fail to make the distinction between the genuine exercise of a virtue and the skillful use of the behavior required for a virtue, MacIntyre's response is inadequate. MacIntyre does not spell out *how* we should distinguish those two, principally because he pays insufficient attention to the fact that the virtues are dispositions of *character* toward feeling and thinking as well as acting. Attention to the formation of character, rather than simply the acquisition of virtues, moves the primary focus away from practices *qua* practices and toward the specification of the friendships in and through which character should be formed. Practices remain important, but only insofar as they are contextualized within an account of friendship.

MacIntyre does recognize that relationships are necessary for practices and hence acquiring and exercising the virtues. He writes,

> Every practice requires a certain kind of relationship between those who participate in it. Now the virtues are those goods by reference to which, whether we like it or not, we define our relationships to those other people with whom we share the kind of purposes and standards which inform practices.[5]

Even more, MacIntyre contends that particular kinds of relationships are themselves practices: the varieties of ways in which forms of human community are made and sustained can qualify as practices.

This suggests that the kind of formation that occurs through practices entails not only a person's formation through activities but also, and more determinatively, a formation that occurs through the friendships that precede those activities, arise out of those activities, or are themselves constitutive of those activities. Unfortunately, MacIntyre does not develop an account of these attachments. On his own terms, when he is explicating the Aristotelian tradition, he rather curiously omits the central importance Aristotle attributes to *philia*, normally translated as friendship. Moreover, when he turns in *Whose Justice? Which Rationality?* to defending "a version of the Augustinian tradition" whose high point is Thomas Aquinas, MacIntyre fails to recognize the importance of friendship with God in Thomas's account of the moral life.

The attachments of friendship, paradigmatically friendship with God, are crucial for the formation and transformation of a person's character. But that does not mean that practices are unrelated to such friendships; indeed they are closely related. Thus it is important to sketch three ways in which friendships can be related to practices: friendships which involve attachments antecedent to any specific practices, friendships which arise out of practices, and friendships which are themselves constitutive of a practice.

The vocation of parenting within Christianity (but by no means confined to Christianity) suggests that the primary friendship that exists antecedent to any particular practice is that found in the relations between parents and children.[6] Parents and children develop a bond of friendship that fosters a sense of belonging.[7] In such a friendship, the parent attempts to guide the child's development; as the child develops, the attachment based on the early sense of belonging can become a full and mutual friendship if, and insofar as, the child comes to see that she is the object of her parents' manifest affections.

There are thus two poles in the development of parent-child friendships: one looking retrospectively back to the child's birth and/or earlier days, and one looking prospectively toward the child's development in becoming a person. To the extent that parents are exemplars of practical wisdom, they will cultivate similar capacities in their children. Likewise, children's desires to form their passions, to learn to act rightly and excellently, and to develop their reason and understanding are bound up with their desire to emulate those they esteem and to cultivate those aspects of character which are exemplified.

I have focused on one understanding of the parent-child relationship for three reasons: first, it is the purest example of a friendship that exists antecedent to practices and one which is important to a Christian understanding of the parental vocation; second, as the primary bond a child may have, the parent-child relationship often has considerable impact on the child's moral formation (or malformation); and third, human beings are children of a Triune God who, Christians claim, befriends and guides them toward becoming persons. I could have focused on other examples of this kind of friendship; other friendships may be found and formed apart from shared practices, though they are more difficult to isolate for description. People discover friends in a variety of ways, and many of these are unrelated (at least in their initial stages) to specific practices.

These attachments, however they are discovered, are crucial for moral formation. They are the kinds of relationships which form people to feel, act, and think in particular ways rather than others. As such, it is important to note that while these friendships are formed apart from specific practices, they are not typically sustained unless shared practices develop. It is not that the shared practices are instrumental to sustaining the friendship; rather the friends who love each other and seek to emulate each other will want to spend time together. And they will spend such time typically by engaging in shared practices which are both a good of the friendship and a means whereby the friends continue to be formed.

There are also friendships that arise out of practices that are important for moral formation. In such cases, people may not know each other prior to sharing in an activity. However, learning to participate in the activities of a practice involves an apprenticeship from others who are, at least ideally, exemplars. The master-apprentice relationship is crucial to the practice, and it creates a context in which a friendship of a particular kind can be developed.

Robert Wilken provides an interesting example of how such relationships are related to practices in his discussion of the Alexandrian "school" in early Christianity.

According to Wilken, Gregory Thaumaturgus's studies under Origen were designed to provide moral and spiritual formation through various practices, particularly the interpretation of Scripture. Through the practices of his study with Origen, Gregory also developed a friendship with his teacher. As Wilken characterizes it,

> Gregory is speaking about spiritual direction, but it is significant that he calls it 'friendship' *(philia)*. Friendship, he says, is "not something one can easily resist, it is piercing and penetrating, an affable and affectionate disposition which is shown in the [teacher's] words and his association with us." Through Origen, Gregory learned to love the Word "whose beauty attracts irresistibly," but he also began to love Origen as well, "the friend and interpreter" of the Word.[8]

In the friendships that are formed out of such practices as the study of Scripture, moral formation (or, as Wilken describes it, "training in virtue") occurs. Such friendships provide a history of shared judgments.[9]

Thus far I have considered two types of friendship: those that exist antecedent to practices and those that arise out of practices. These should not be seen as mutually exclusive alternatives; rather they are ends on a continuum. There are friendships that arise out of practices which then develop into more durable primary attachments independent of any particular practice.[10]

There is a danger, however, in these two examples. I have been describing parent-child and master-apprentice friendships which occur in situations where learning and formation are primary and necessary activities. It might appear that friendship is of only instrumental value. What remains, then, is to spell out how friendship, and paradigmatically friendship with God, is intrinsic to a flourishing life, and how within the context of such friendships moral formation and growth continue to occur.

Friendship can itself be a practice with goods internal to the practice for at least three reasons. First, because human beings only come to be fully persons in relationship, people need others to share goods, interests, and ends in a jointly pursued life. Second, friends are important in helping to provide the self-knowledge necessary for wise judgment. And third, intimate friendships extend and redefine the boundaries of conceptions of how we ought to live.

Because human beings are constituted the way we are, the moral life needs to include provision for a considerable range of activities shared with others—or at least, in the case of those ascetics for whom friendship is focused intensely in relation to God, with an Other. As John Cooper summarizes it, "Only by merging one's activities and interests with those of others can the inherent fragility of any human being's interests be overcome."[11] Earlier I suggested that friendship is necessary for specifying the place of the virtues in practices; here it becomes apparent that the relationship is reciprocal, that practices are necessary for sustaining friendships.

This account needs further development in order to sustain the larger claim that friendship is crucial to the moral life. It is not just that people share in activities with others, find those activities to be important to their lives, and value the persons with whom they are engaging in the activities. Rather those with whom one shares in practices will influence who she will become; thus it is not enough simply to engage in practices with others, it is important to be aware of the character of these others such that one is willing to have her own character interwoven with theirs.

This points to the second reason that friendship can itself be a practice; it is through friends that one comes to know oneself. It is exceedingly difficult for people to attain objectivity about their own actions and character; people tend to point out faults in others while overlooking their own, and they tend to attribute to themselves non-existent virtues. Overcoming self-deception and acquiring self-knowledge is an extremely difficult task.

Friends are crucial to self-knowledge in several ways. First, as a result of similarities, a friend may serve as a "second self" who is a mirror for discerning one's own character.[12] Second, and more determinatively for a Christian account, a friend may contribute to self-knowledge not through similarities but through differences. Such differences may be occasioned by inequalities in the development of the virtues, but differences may also result from the possibility of a diversity of ideals of virtuous characters. Even granting the interrelation of the virtues, the pattern of virtues might be, and indeed will be, different in different persons. In this case, one learns about oneself by contrast with others. In theological terms, a person's primary friendship is with the Triune God who is decisively Other and is, in turn, embodied in a community (i.e., the Body of Christ) in which the diversity of gifts and characters are celebrated.

A third role for friends in acquiring self-knowledge is the critical perspective they have on a person's life which she herself often lacks. Friends often see a person less deceptively than she is able to see herself and they can help her to be less dishonest about her life. Their observations are helpful in minimizing her own tendencies toward self-deception. They can help interpret what was going on in a particular situation, and they can locate the gaps between her avowals of who she is and what they observe her to have done.

In addition to this critical function, however, they also foster self-knowledge in positive ways. They sometimes perceive growth one may not have noticed. Because friends share conceptions of the ends toward which one's life is directed, they help her see how her life is related to those ends.

Even more, and perhaps most comprehensively, friends are important for helping a person to narrate her life in such a way as to see its complex unity (though not uniformity).[13] Sometimes a person's life is subjected to so much fragmentation and so much chaos that she can lose her way and sense that she has lost the integrated focus which gave her life direction. In such cases friends who have known the person for a long time can discern continuities in her projects and her priorities. Such a friend or friends can help to provide an alternative narrative to the one which has left the person feeling caught in chaos.

Because the narrative of a person's life is inextricably tied to others' narratives—and most influentially the narratives of her friends' lives—self-knowledge requires the recognition that, in MacIntyre's phrase, people are at most (and often, particularly in modern societies, much less than) the "co-authors" of their narratives. MacIntyre goes on:

> I am not only accountable, I am one who can always ask others for an account, who can put others to the question. I am part of their story, as they are part of mine. The narrative of any one life is part of an interlocking set of narratives. Moreover this asking for and giving of accounts itself plays an important part in constituting narratives.[14]

Hence conversations with friends are essential for self-knowledge, for it is through seeing how people's lives are interrelated that they can learn to narrate their own lives less deceptively and less incoherently.

Friends thus provide a mutual apprenticeship in virtue, for a person's life and her observations provide friends with greater self-knowledge in the same ways they do for her. Through spending time together, people are enabled to come to know themselves. They are enabled to see as their friends see, think as they think, act as they act, as they also come to appreciate the ways in which their friends will forever be separate and distinct selves whose lives are different from their own. Thus friendship is a good in that it is important for the self-knowledge that is integral to being a person of character.

The third reason the moral life needs the practice of friendship is because intimate friendships extend and redefine the boundaries of particular conceptions of how we ought to live. Friendship involves growing morally and becoming virtuous in ways that form and deepen people's lives, their conceptions of their ends, and the friendship itself.

Part of the practice of friendship involves a conversation about the divergent ways in which even people of practical wisdom evaluate particular situations and issues. As Nancy Sherman suggests,

> Through collaboration on projects and through listening to and identifying with the viewpoints of others, an agent's vision becomes expanded and enlarged. The agent comes to learn different ways of reading a situation and different questions to pose in order to see the picture with increased insight and clarity. How to see becomes as much a matter of inquiry as what to do.[15]

Hence the differences which exist among friends are significant because the disagreements become occasions for extending conversation and inquiry about who people are and what they should do. Or, as I shall describe it with reference to Christian community, it suggests that there will be an ongoing "puzzlement" about what following Jesus and living in the mystery of the Triune God entails.[16]

People ought to want to have a diversity of friends. Because each friend possesses qualities that are distinct from oneself, and typically from one's other friends, such diversity ought to enhance the conversation while extending and deepening one's vision. Sometimes a person's vision is extended in that she includes features she had not seen before; it also happens—in cases of unresolved disagreement—that people's vision is deepened by clarifying the nature of the disagreement. But both in the extension and the deepening of vision, diversity within the community of friends (if it is genuinely a community where goods are held in common) is desirable because it stimulates conversation among friends; and such stimulating conversation extends and deepens the shared vision, develops character, and enhances people's capacity to make wise judgments.

So friendship, which is constitutive of a kind of community, is itself a practice which is integral to the moral life. Friendship is integral because (1) human life is fundamentally relational, (2) people come to know themselves through friends, and (3) the community that emerges provides a conversation through which particular conceptions of how people ought to live are redefined and extended. The practice of friendship is both indispensable to moral formation and an important constituent of the moral life itself.

Friendships, practices, and the practices of friendship provide interrelated contexts which form and/or malform people in moral judgment. But what is crucial are not friendships and practices *per se*, but the specific friendships and practices of Christian living in relation to the Triune God. In particular, I will argue that humanity is called to a friendship with the Triune God, and that such friendship provides a distinctive shaping to the moral life. Christian claims about God and humanity reveal not only the possibility of humanity having a friendship with God but also the importance of so doing if people are to be formed and transformed in wise moral judgment. Thus it is to an exploration of the relationship between God's Trinity and humanity's vocation that I now turn.

2.2 THE MYSTERY OF GOD'S TRINITY AND THE STRUGGLE TO BECOME PERSONS

In order to understand the depiction of God as Triune that I am providing, it is important to make an initial distinction between "grammar" and "description" in talk about God.[17] A grammatical account does not purport to offer a proper account of the subject in question; rather it attempts to discourage improper ones. So in talk about God, a grammatical account does not attempt to claim what or who God is; it takes the "picture" of God grounded in specific religious practices such as worship, and its role is

> to exercise critical watch over it, now unraveling confusions and inconsistencies that arise from it, now checking it with *praxis* to offset its stereotypical drift, now challenging it as lazy simplification.[18]

By contrast, a descriptive account purports to provide a proper account; in discussion about God, such an account claims to furnish some direct description of the mystery of God.

While the distinction between "grammar" and "description" is somewhat overdrawn and will need to be qualified in later discussion, it nonetheless is important. The claim, often made within the Christian tradition, that God is mystery is, in the first instance, an insistence on the inappropriateness of a descriptive account. There is an absolute qualitative difference between infinite and finite which compels a posture of agnosticism about the character of God. At some point humanity is reduced to silence, confessing the transcendence and utter incomprehensibility of God.

But that is not to suggest that construing God as mystery is the only way Christians talk about God. Two other construals are worth noting. First, there are theologians and philosophers who dispute the claim that

God is mystery and attempt to provide direct descriptions of God through a list of attributes. There are remarkable difficulties with such attempts, but nonetheless they persist. The persistence is partially explained by the felt need to defend "theism" against a particular form of atheism derived from the Enlightenment.[19] Second, some Christian theologians who accept the claim that God is mystery think that is the end of appropriate talk about God. That is to say, they think that agnosticism is the *only* appropriate attitude.

The first strategy, that of denying the mystery of God by offering a general description of God, not only has philosophical and theological difficulties in providing defensible warrants for the description. The God of theism, thus described in terms of attributes of "godness," is not the God of Jesus Christ. To begin with a general account of the attributes of "godness," (i.e., to provide a general description of God) and then subsequently to "fill in" and "complicate" that simple description by consideration of God's Trinity, is to misunderstand the Christian doctrine of the Triune God.

The problem with the second strategy (at least for Christian theologians), namely recommending agnosticism as the *only* appropriate attitude, lies in its rejection of the doctrine of the Trinity. God is not only transcendent in ways that compel awe, silence, and questioning, God is immanent through the self-gift of Jesus Christ and the power of the Holy Spirit. While Christian trinitarian doctrine is not—at least should not be—an attempt to describe God, it is essential as the "summary grammar" of the mystery of salvation.

Nicholas Lash makes an important distinction between agnosticism as a religious attitude and as a theological policy.

> We need to distinguish between agnosticism as a religious attitude (the practical attitude of one who refrains

from worship because of his suspicion that songs of
praise are sung not merely into silence but into empti-
ness) and as a theological policy aimed at insistently
reminding the believer of the limits both of his language
and of his theoretical understanding.[20]

Hence the assertion that God is mystery is grounded
not in a "religious" but in a "theological" agnosticism.
A properly theological agnosticism recognizes the centrality of the doctrine of the Trinity as the proper "grammar" about God, while insisting nonetheless that such
a "grammar" does not provide a direct description of
God.

However, the distinction between grammar and description should not be overdrawn. Christian "grammar" about God includes truth-claims about who God
is and what the world is like. Disciplined attention to
linguistic usage in prayer, praise, and other Christian
practices can *show* something of the character of humanity's relationship to God and hence informs Christian
discourse about God. After all, Christians believe that
the God who is and remains mystery nevertheless has
created humanity, has spoken to humanity through a
"*self*-statement in the flesh and texture of our history,"
and has provided an "imperishable *self*-gift."[21]

Putting it in this manner, then, suggests the way in
which it is perfectly intelligible to speak of human destiny as "participating in the mystery of God." Because
of God's self-statement and self-gift through Jesus
Christ in the Holy Spirit, humanity can be said to know
something about God and, in particular, about humanity's relationship to God.

How does a Christian claim that humanity can be said
to know something about the God who is mystery? The
first step can be made by a consideration of human love.
The knowledge that is born of human love is frequently,
if not always, incapable of being brought to adequate

expression. But the lover does not infer from her inability to describe (i.e., to bring to language) the beloved that the beloved is thus not known. As Nicholas Lash suggests,

> The 'reticence' of the lover, his continual negation of expressions perceived as inadequate to their object, does not argue nescience, but a more penetrating knowledge than that contained in those 'neutral' descriptions of the beloved that are also available to casual acquaintances, and are found in the files of the family doctor and the social historian.[22]

Hence on this view knowledge of God is discovered in and through an ever-deepening intimate relationship characterized by Thomas Aquinas as "friendship with God."

But a second step also must be made. Human love is always threatened by illusion and by self-deception about the beloved. Such illusion and deception can be rooted either in the individual or in social constructions that mask reality. Thus even more serious is the threat of illusion and self-deception posed in humanity's personal knowledge of the unknown God. In this light the importance of the grammatical account involving the corrective purification of illusion and distortion of talk about God becomes even more apparent.

One of the central claims of the Christian tradition has been that "God is love." Such a claim is not based on any abstract or sentimental notions about love; rather it is connected to the history of God's love expressed through God's activities of creation, redemption, and sustenance. That history finds its expression in the doctrine of the Trinity. As Rowan Williams suggests,

> 'God reveals himself' means that the meaning of the word 'God' establishes itself among us as the loving and nurturing advent of *newness* in human life—grace, for-

giveness, empowerment to be the agents of forgiveness
and liberation. This advent has its centre, its normative
focus, in the record of Jesus; it occurs among us now as
the re-presentation of Jesus through the Spirit; and it
rests upon and gives content to the fundamental regulative notion of initiative, creative or generative power,
potentiality, that is not circumscribed by the conditions
of the empirical world—the *arche* of the Father, the ultimate source.[23]

The God who is love reveals that love in self-communication, a self-communication which enables the worship
and affirmation of God as "Father, Son, and Holy
Spirit" and which calls forth from people a life of love
in responsive friendship with God.[24]

Hence understanding God as Trinity is closely connected to a particular way of life, a life of discipleship.
As Lash expresses it,

> Christianity is, itself, a 'way,' a school of discipleship,
> the grammar of whose pedagogy is expressed, in sum-
> mary form, in the doctrine of the Trinity.[25]

Christian discipleship amounts to a schooling whereby
people learn, in the context of learning to understand
God as Trinity, how they are to live and what judgments they are to make. In short, God includes the
creation in God's own life, and that inclusion enables
humanity to participate in the mystery of God.

Such a view, one which affirms a particular place for
humanity in God's purposes, need not be "anthropocentric" in the sense James Gustafson finds objection-
able.[26] For example, Lash argues that humanity's encounter with the Triune God consists in the responsible
and effective recognition of human creatureliness, of
human finitude. In particular, he contends that God is
to be found in the limits of the ordinary, and that a
Christian account of God will be marked by friction and

instability as each affirmation will require correction by other affirmations as are prompted by other dimensions of human life.[27]

On this basis, Lash suggests that the doctrine of God's Trinity, as it is confessed in the Creed, not only indicates where God is to be found in human life but also prevents people from ever assuming that what is found there can be simply identified with God.[28] For example, in action and discourse patterned by the frame of reference provided by the Creed, Lash contends that people "learn to find God in all life, all freedom, all creativity and vitality, and in each fresh particular beauty, each unexpected attainment of relationship and community—for all such occurrences are forms of his presence."[29] Ascribing all creativity and conversion, all fresh life and freedom, to divinity is a way of insisting that there is nothing "outside" the presence of God. Hence the doctrine of God as Spirit is discovered. But to stop with such an affirmation would result in pantheism. Though the instinct of pantheism is sound, namely its insistence that God is not some entity outside the world, it nonetheless "obscures the difference between the world and God, mistakes the sign and promise for the reality, and thereby leads us disastrously to misread our circumstances and responsibilities."[30]

Pantheism, Lash suggests, is rendered implausible by the brokenness of the world. There is too much contingency and fragility, too much pain and chaos, too much perishing of beauty and significance; this brokenness is incomprehensible and silences any celebration. Thus those who latch onto Spirit as the nature of God are liable to be caught in various forms of idolatry. What is needed is the corrective insistence on the absolute *difference* between God and the world. As Lash suggests,

> In the pain and confusion, the darkness and inhumanity, the egotism and uncontrollable destructiveness which

surround us (and to which we contribute, whether energetically or by practical indifference), it is not too difficult to learn that that to which the word 'God' refers is unimaginable, unknowable, ungraspable.[31]

Here, where the limits of action and the impotence of understanding are reached, people are led to a stance of questioning—perhaps even reduced to silence. But to stop there would result in agnosticism or atheism. The instinct of agnosticism is sound, Lash suggests, in its reminder that the mystery of God is incomprehensible. Even so, to latch onto agnosticism (or many forms of atheism) ends up indirectly producing idolatry because "it seems as if we *have* to set our hearts on *something*, and if we find ourselves unable to acknowledge, in basic trust, our absolute dependence, then what we do, in resolute assertion of autonomy, is in fact to *divinize*—to ascribe divine or absolute significance to—ourselves or our plans or our possessions or some feature of our world."[32]

Thus the silence and questioning requires the corrective insistence on God's Word, the "rule of speech and action which furnishes us with the pattern or figure according to which we are able to *correlate* the doctrines of origin and gift, creator and spirit." As people learn to shape their speech and, more importantly, their lives in relation to "one Word once spoken in one life lived and one death undergone," as they recognize that people are to relate with one another "in communion" with the risen one, people are enabled to sustain the dialectic between atheism and pantheism, denial and affirmation, indifference and fanaticism.[33]

Even so, or perhaps particularly so, Christians have found it all too easy to latch onto the specificity of God's work in Jesus Christ and to assume that they now have *possession* of all truth and have laid hold of the nature of God. When that is done, when the language and particular institutions which mediate the memory of Jesus are "divinized," people make the mistake of ascribing absolute significance to the past *as* past.

Yet once again the doctrine of God's Trinity contains within itself the necessary corrective resources. On the one hand, the insistence on God's incomprehensibility serves as a reminder that though people confess the Word as God, speech ought never come too easily. People ought to remember, so Lash insists, that the utterance is not the utterer, that "though he is 'God of God' and 'light of light,' the light illuminated in the clarification which he supplies remains (for us) impenetrable darkness which is not more dispelled for us than it was for him in Gethsemane." On the other hand, the insistence on God's gift and possibility serves as a reminder that the task of mediating the memory of Jesus and enabling communion with the risen Christ rests not in the clutches of human institutions ascribed divine status but in God's gracious hands. According to Lash, the burden laid upon human beings in discipleship of Jesus Christ, namely the task of constituting community in the Spirit and of bearing witness to the possibility of such community for all of humankind, may be undertaken in tranquility in the assurance that "God himself is all finitude's inmost gift and possibility."[34]

Overall, Lash contends the dance, the "perichoresis," of Christian discipleship proceeds in such an interaction.[35] In the encounter with God which consists in the acknowledgment of human creatureliness and finitude, it is never and nowhere appropriate to "stop the dance," to interrupt the dialectic of human life and to say: "*this* and this alone is what we mean by 'God'; *here* and here alone is his presence and activity to be discerned."[36]

It is important to specify (in ways Lash does not, and perhaps would not) that learning to live in the pattern of God's Trinity occurs in and through the practices of

Christian communities. Christian communities are the carriers of such language about, and depictions of, the Triune God and God's relations to human life. Because of the recurring temptations to conceptual neatness and theoretical resolution, it is crucial to remember that such communities must maintain the practice of an ongoing vigilance against corruptions of language and distortions of the dialectics of human life. Language about God is specified in the flux of action and interpretation in the life of Christian communities. While the pedagogies of Christian discipleship receive their summary grammar from a particular depiction of God as Triune, the shape of that discipleship is significantly determined both by the moral health of the friendships and practices in and through which that depiction is learned and by the theological clarity with which that depiction is sustained.

The claim that Christian discipleship receives its summary grammar from the doctrine of the Trinity suggests that there is a correlative view of "personhood" to the depiction of God as Triune. On this view, what makes human beings "persons" cannot be equated with any one feature or element from the complex and bewildering manifold that constitutes human life. One way of attempting to isolate personhood is to turn to a feature such as rationality as that which separates persons from, for example, animals; such a view has been subjected to penetrating critique by Mary Midgley.[37] Another way of attempting to do so is by designating personhood as that which is ineluctably mine; what constitutes me as a person is my private experiences (i.e., my "personal" existence) which stand over-against the public world. Wittgenstein's arguments against private language have made such a view difficult to defend.[38]

In contrast, the view I am developing suggests that "persons" are what humans may hope and must struggle to become. Personhood is not what humans initially, privately, and "inwardly" are, nor is it some feature that distinguishes humans from other creatures such as rationality (or, alternatively, feelings). To be a person is not to have some kind of "stuff," a substance that is amenable to description like a finger or a toe; rather it denotes, as I suggested in chapter one, the capacity to *narrate* the circumstances of human life via an autobiography.

Such narration entails the recognition (1) that humans are social beings, (2) that unity comes only on the other side of complexity, (3) that there can be no sharp divorce between reason and the passions, and (4) that people's identities are shaped as much by what happens to them as by what they do. Those claims can now be situated more properly with reference to the Christian account of God's Trinity. The insistence that humans are social beings is a reminder that, while it is certainly important in some contexts to focus on human nature in terms of biological constitution (for example, as a way of protesting against the exclusion of various groups such as Jews, blacks, slaves, women, unborn babies, etc., from the realm of personhood), such a focus is never sufficient. Our identities are forged in and through particular social contexts. As Lash argues, "the nature of the human is never completely *given*, in biological constitution or historical achievement, but has again and again to be sought and struggled for, in action, affection, agreement, and understanding."[39]

The other three claims receive their specification with reference to the perichoretic dance of discipleship patterned in God's Trinity. There is no way to become a person except through interaction with the various people, forces, and factors which make up the world. That calls on both reason and the passions, it involves both what people do and what is done to them, and it requires willingness to confront the complexities of an often confusing, fragmentary, and conflictual world.

Thus persons are what humans hope to become in the measure that they are able to "balance in tension" the complex factors and forces that constitute human life in the world; and that requires a struggle, a continual, practical, costly, and precarious quest.

Human identity is continually both under threat and under construction. Various features converge either to destruct human identities or to help construct them, and it requires both an individual and a social struggle to eliminate that which destroys and to enhance that which builds.[40] As Lash suggests, given that the "whole complex, conflictual, unstable process of human history is a matter of the production and destruction of the 'personal'," Christianity has a threefold witness: it "at once discloses that this *is* the character of the process, serves as a 'school for the production of the personal'— a school whose pedagogy is structured in suffering— and promises that process's eventual achievement."[41]

It is in and through the friendships and practices of Christian communities, and paradigmatically through the practice of friendship with the Triune God, that the "production of the personal" is given its specific shape. That is, a Christian account of formation and transformation in moral judgment receives its shape and context in the specification of how belief in God as Triune carries with it a distinctive perspective on what it means to become a person.

In the terms developed thus far, the central affirmation of Christian life is that God has graciously enabled humanity to participate in the mystery of the Triune God, and that by so participating human beings are schooled in a discipleship that sets them on the way to becoming persons. Hence the task of Christian life is to learn, in response to God's grace, to live a life in friendship with the Triune God manifested in the perichoretic dance of discipleship. Enabling such learning is the task of the pedagogies of Christian discipleship, pedagogies

grounded in the "summary grammar" of the depiction
of God as Triune and whose structure of specific friendships and practices provide a distinctive shaping to
Christian life and a distinctive perspective on the activity of moral judgment.

Providing an account of the pedagogies of Christian
discipleship will be the focus of the third chapter. Before
turning to such an account, however, I set the context
by outlining how "friendship" with the Triune God calls
forth a response of transformative discipleship.

2.3 GOD'S FRIENDSHIP AND TRANSFORMATIVE DISCIPLESHIP

Since God has included the creation within God's life,
participating in the mystery of the Triune God is not
only possible but is necessary for becoming persons.
On the basis of what God has done for humanity, and
in particular on the basis of God's own self-statement
and self-gift in Jesus Christ, it is possible to speak mean-
ingfully not only of knowing the mystery of God, but
of being friends of God.

Such a claim sounds rather odd; even if I have suc-
ceeded in showing that people can participate in the
mystery of God, it seems absurd to carry that one step
further and to characterize that participation as a kind
of friendship. In what sense, then, is Christian life—a
life characterized by discipleship—best understood as a
friendship with the Triune God? Two references in the
New Testament provide significant clues.

The first is found in Luke 7:34.[42] There Jesus, in com-
paring himself to John the Baptist, describes his own
activity: "The Son of man has come eating and drinking;
and you say, 'Behold, a glutton and a drunkard, a friend
of tax collectors and sinners!'" The term "friend of tax
collectors and sinners" was meant as a contemptuous,

derogatory reference; Jesus was not playing by the rules of "respectable" society. But ironically this contemptuous name unintentionally expresses an important truth about Jesus' ministry. Jesus befriends people wherever he encounters them, and in particular he befriends those excluded and marginalized by "established" society and the "conventional" powers: the poor, the sick, the outcast. As friend, Jesus is God's friendship; in particular, he reveals God's friendship to those who have been treated in an "unfriendly" fashion by society.

The second passage is found in the Gospel of John; in being called to follow Jesus as his disciples, people are not merely being conscripted into his service; they are invited to become his friends (John 15:15). When Jesus declares himself to be the friend of the disciples, he also calls them into a new life of friendship. Upon recognizing that this Jesus is none other than God's own self-expression, it becomes apparent that God desires to be present with and for humanity in a relationship of friendship. David Burrell's comments are instructive:

> An invitation to friendship with divinity taxes our credulity, so much so that to accept it *is* to believe Christianly. That seemingly impossible barrier being breached, it is a relatively small step to speak of intimacy with God—both as individuals and as a people, for this God has already acknowledged delight in being with us. The capacity of divinity to delight in us creates in its turn an entirely new dimension of receptivity in us.[43]

Friendship with God is a way of speaking of God's desire to be in relationship with humanity. God, who has *always* been humanity's friend, through Christ enables people to become God's friends. Christian discipleship is to be grounded in responsive friendship with the God of Jesus Christ who enables that discipleship through the power of the Holy Spirit, and growth in discipleship is directed toward an ever-deepening friendship with God whereby people also befriend others. That is to say, while the practice of friendship is central to a depiction of formation in moral judgment, for Christians it is a specific friendship, namely the practice of friendship with God, which provides the paradigmatic context for formation and transformation in moral judgment.

In this section I will first explore St. Thomas Aquinas's explication of the grammatical significance of friendship with God for Christian life and discipleship. Then I will explore several issues surrounding the specific shape of the transformative discipleship which characterizes the Christian's friendship with God.

2.31 St. Thomas on Friendship with God

According to Thomas the Christian life is a life of friendship, fundamentally a life of ever-deepening intimacy with God whereby Christians participate more fully in the happiness of God. Humanity was created that people might attain the beatific vision in friendship with God. Friendship with God entails the recognition that humanity's *telos* is to come to see God not only as One who is good to humanity, but as the One in whose friendship people can become persons.

Thomas's account of friendship is indebted to Aristotle's, but whereas for Aristotle friendship with the gods is impossible because the inequality is so great and because the gods lie outside the *telos* of human life, for Thomas friendship with God is at the heart of Christian life. Thus Thomas had to show that because of God's self-gift in Jesus Christ, friendship with God both is made possible and is humanity's vocation.

Thomas had to deal with an important theological objection: in the fall and the resultant existence of sin, humanity lost (at least in large measure) the possibility of friendship with God.

> Sin has two phases, the turning to transient advantage, and the consequent turning away from God. Punishment corresponds to both, for, first, a man is hurt by the shortcomings of the things he has chosen to give him pleasure, and, secondly, *he has lost grace and the other gifts of God's friendship.*[44]

Inasmuch as sin does not completely destroy human nature, friendship is still possible (although not, presumably, with God) in some sense.[45] Yet even though friendship with God is damaged by sin, God remains a friend to humanity.

For Thomas, the moral life does not begin in a neutral position before God. A Christian begins as a sinner, as a person turned away from God and toward himself. Becoming a friend of God thus requires a transformation, which is dependent on God's enablement of friendship by reconciling humanity to God. Such is the context of God's gift of grace,[46] and suggests the importance of Christology for understanding friendship with God. Before examining the shape of the Christian's transformation, it is important to explore what it means to be befriended by God.

Thomas focuses on two ways in which God befriends humanity; through Christ's atoning work, and through Christ's continuing presence in the sacraments. Thomas uses the image of friendship as a means of articulating what Jesus did for human salvation.

> What our friends do and endure on our behalf are in a sense our own deeds and sufferings, for friendship is a mutual power uniting two persons and making them somehow one: for this reason a man be justly discharged because his friend has made restitution.[47]

Or, as he puts it in the *Summa,* "When two persons live in friendship, one may make satisfaction for the other."[48]

The claim Thomas makes is that although in its sinfulness humanity has lost the gifts of God's friendship, God befriends humanity in Jesus Christ.

> By suffering in order to save us Christ conferred benefits on us over and above the mere escaping from sin. First, because now we realize how much God loves us, and now we can be roused to love him in return; this friendship is the heart of spiritual health.[49]

As humanity's friend (whom God has given in grace), Christ is able (both in his life and in his death) to restore humanity to friendship with God.

The role of Christ is mediator, the one in fellowship with whom humanity is reconciled to the God from whom its sin had left it estranged. As Thomas puts it, "Christ alone is the perfect Mediator of God and men, since by His death He reconciled the human race to God."[50] Christ's cross is the point of mediation because in dying for his enemies and forgiving them, Jesus— who is God's friendship-love—makes them God's friends. The cross reestablishes the likeness or similarity people need to be God's friends. But becoming God's friends also calls forth a life of discipleship, a life patterned in Jesus Christ.[51] For Thomas, while the cross is the means whereby humanity is reconciled to God and is thus enabled to have friendship with God, Christ's atonement demands the response of a life of discipleship patterned in Christ.

Before moving to a discussion of the shape of that discipleship, however, there is another dimension crucial to Thomas's explication. Thomas contends that Christian life is centered in friendship with God; but friendship, particularly as it is explicated by Aristotle, requires mutuality, and Jesus was an historical figure whom Christians affirm has now been exalted to "the right hand of God the Father." Thus if Thomas wants to claim that friendship with God remains for humanity *here and now* a continuing possibility in any meaningful sense, he needs to describe the means by which God continues to be present to humanity. It is in this context that the continuing presence of Christ in the sacraments becomes crucial.

According to Thomas it is in the Church, and preeminently in the sacraments, that people continue to experience Christ's presence. In particular, the eucharist is the center of sacramental life. As Thomas puts it, Christ is really present in the eucharist, and is thus the culmination of all the other sacraments in which his power is shared.[52]

Moreover, Thomas contends Christ is really present in the eucharist in the manner of his *passion*. Thus it is in the eucharist where the friendship with God restored in Christ's passion is made continually present to humanity. As Thomas construes it, the eucharist is the sacrament of the passion of Christ;[53] as it was Christ's passion which restored humanity to friendship with God, so the eucharist is "the sacrament of charity."[54]

In the eucharist humanity is given a "proof of friendship, that [Christ] should feed us himself. . . ."[55] In the *Summa* Thomas makes the relation between Christ's presence in the eucharist and God's befriending of humanity even more pronounced:

This belongs to Christ's love, out of which for our salvation He assumed a true body of our nature. And because it is the special feature of friendship to live together with friends, as the Philosopher says [*Nicomachean Ethics* ix], He promises us His bodily presence as a reward, saying (Matth. xxiv.28): *Where the body is, there shall the eagles be gathered together.* Yet meanwhile in our pilgrimage He does not deprive us of His bodily pres-

ence; but unites us with Himself in this sacrament
through the truth of His body and blood. Hence (John
vi.57) he says: *He that eateth My flesh, and drinketh My
blood, abideth in Me, and I in him.* Hence this sacrament
is the sign of supreme charity, and the uplifter of our
hope, from such familiar union of Christ with us.[56]

In the eucharist, according to Thomas, the participants
feed on Christ. Thomas's distinction between bodily
and spiritual food makes the significance of feeding on
Christ even more prominent.

Bodily food is changed into the substance of the person
who eats it and, therefore, is of no help in conserving
life unless it is physically consumed. . . . Spiritual food
changes man into itself. This is the teaching of
Augustine in his *Confessions.* He heard, as it were, the
voice of Christ saying to him, *You will not change me into
yourself as you would the food of your flesh; but you will be
changed into me.*[57]

Elsewhere Thomas says that the habit of charity is kindled
by receiving the eucharist.[58] Thus for Thomas to feed
on Christ is gradually to lose the old, sinful self in order
to be changed into a new self, a Christlike friend of God.

Hence in Thomas's account, the eucharist is the sacrament of the passion, the restoration of humanity's
friendship with God and the means by which people
learn what form their discipleship is to take. The eucharist preserves people from the sin that separates them
from God,[59] and it provides the nourishment necessary
for the journey toward perfect friendship with God.[60]

Thus it is that, on the basis of Christ's work and his
continuing presence in the sacraments, humanity is
conformed to Christ such that people are enabled to be,
and to become, friends of God. Being so conformed is
inseparable from, and is the central prerequisite of, a life
of discipleship.

One aspect of this discipleship is described by Thomas in his discussion of charity. According to Thomas, charity is best understood as friendship with God.[61] That is the primary thrust of question 23 of the *Secunda Secundae*. But even earlier, in the *Prima Secundae*, Thomas had written: "Charity signifies not only the love of God but also a certain friendship with Him; and this implies, besides love, a certain mutual return of love, together with mutual communion, as stated in the *Ethics*."[62] Thus Thomas aims to articulate the relationship a Christian has with God as a friendship; the love God has for people and that people have for God is properly expressed as the love friends share.

Thomas suggests that the communication that establishes friendship between humans and God is God sharing with humanity God's very happiness.[63] But in what does God's happiness consist? Thomas indicates that it is the friendship among the persons of the Trinity. For God to be happy is for God to be God, and for Thomas this means being a Trinity of friendship. Thus what God communicates when God "befriends" humanity through grace is the friendship life which is God. Thomas writes,

> Charity is a friendship of man for God, founded upon the fellowship of everlasting happiness. Now this fellowship is in respect, not of natural, but of gratuitous gifts, for, according to Rom. vi.23, *the grace of God is life everlasting:* Therefore charity itself surpasses our natural faculties. . . . Therefore charity can be in us neither naturally, nor through acquisition by the natural powers, but by the infusion of the Holy Ghost, Who is the love of the Father and the Son, and the participation of Whom in us is created charity.[64]

Hence God befriends humanity through the gift of Jesus Christ, and enables humanity's response of friendship through the Holy Spirit's gift of charity.[65]

In this context it is possible to understand why charity is the form of the virtues. If the discussion of charity is abstracted from its primary locus in friendship with God and its enablement by the Holy Spirit, then it is unclear on what grounds Thomas makes charity the form of the virtues. But that is precisely the point: charity is the form of the virtues not because of any idealization of love, but because a life of friendship with God (which is charity) calls forth a correspondingly specific set of virtues contextualized in specific patterns of discipleship.

However, as Gilbert Meilaender has argued, the language of charity and the language of friendship may not be altogether compatible. In Jeremy Taylor's words, "When friendships were the noblest things in the world, charity was little."[66] Are charity, particularly understood as *agape*, and friendship incompatible? After all, such people as Anders Nygren and Gene Outka have claimed that Christian life is really concerned not with friendship but *agape*.[67]

There is a certain tension between friendship and *agape*.[68] Even so, that tension has been overdrawn and has resulted in a misleading conception of *agape* and of God. It is a mistake to view God's love for God's creatures as being fundamentally impartial. As Helen Oppenheimer argues,

> 'Impartiality' is not a divine virtue, but a human expedient to make up for the limits of our concern on the one hand and the corruptibility of our affections on the other. If we find ourselves neglecting, or spoiling, or abusing, we need to be more even-handed and partiality becomes a vice; but the august partiality of God is a taking hold of the special character of each creature as uniquely significant.[69]

To put it summarily: God is that being whose capacity to love particularly enriches God's capacity to love each particularly.

Hence there need not be a dichotomy between friendship and *agape*. Because people are not God, the call to *agape*, to selfless service to the neighbor, is one which Christians are to fulfill all along their journey. And because of humanity's capacity for harm and injury—because evil continues to reside even in transformed persons—impartiality and impartial love does have an important place in Christian life. But, impartiality is not the goal of Christian life; it is the result of human limitations. The task and goal of Christian life is to grow in friendship with God so that people are increasingly able to see every other human being as loved uniquely by God. The goal of the Christian is to be able to see each and every stranger as a friend *in* God, and as a friend *of* God. Hence ultimately, as Thomas insists, *agape* and friendship are to be coextensive, for only by extending friendship with God into friendship with God's children does human life find its fulfillment.

Thomas further specifies that Christian discipleship in friendship with God is framed by an imitation of Christ. At the start of the *Tertia Pars*, Thomas puts it as follows: "Because our Saviour the Lord Jesus Christ, in order to *save His people from their sins* (Matt. 1:21), as the angel announced, showed to us in His own Person the way of truth whereby we may attain to the bliss of eternal life by rising again. . . ."[70] The goal of the Christian moral life is to make one's way back to God who is humanity's happiness, and it is Jesus Christ who represents the paradigm of Christian discipleship. The following extended quotation is significant for explicating Thomas's thought:

> Hence the Word of God, Who is His eternal concept, is the exemplary likeness of all creatures. And therefore as creatures are established in their proper species though subject to change, by the participation of this likeness, so by the non-participated but personal union

of the Word with a creature it was fitting that the creature should be restored in its order to eternal and un-
changeable perfection; for the craftsman by the intelligible form of his art, whereby he fashioned his handi-
work, restores it when it has fallen into ruin. Moreover,
He has a particular agreement with human nature, since
the Word is the concept of the eternal Wisdom, from
Whom all man's wisdom is derived. And hence man is
perfected in wisdom (which is his proper perfection, as
he is rational) by participating in the Word of God, as
the disciple is instructed by receiving the word of his
master.[71]

Thus humanity is restored to God through Christ, and
as a consequence people are called to pattern their lives
in Christ by becoming disciples instructed by the master. Friendship is perfectly exhibited in God's own trinitarian life; although that perfect friendship cannot be
attained in this life, people are nonetheless called to the
highest perfection humanly possible.[72] Such perfection,
according to Thomas, is dependent on a life of discipleship, centered in charity, and lived in the imitation
of Christ.

2.32 Transformative Discipleship in Friendship with God

How is the life of discipleship best characterized? Three
dimensions of discipleship, particularly as it is connected
to friendship with God, need to be identified and explored. The first is a further clarification of the relationship between what Christ accomplished for human salvation and humanity's response of a particular kind of
life (what might be called, in more traditional terms, the
relationship between "grace" and "virtue"). The second
is the identification of the dialectical relationship between formation and transformation that is occasioned

by conversion to a new way of life. The third is a brief exploration of the content of Christian discipleship, and in particular the question of whether discipleship has a singular pattern or a plurality of paradigms.

The first dimension needs clarification. In chapter one I located a capacity for moral judgment (albeit one that is continually developing) in the continuity of character which gives actions their intelligibility. That suggests that a person's capacity for moral judgment is dependent on her own acquired abilities. Yet being "befriended" by God suggests that the source of the moral life lies outside a person's acquired capacities, and in fact may call those acquired capacities radically into question.

I also suggested that friendship is central to moral formation because, throughout a person's life from early childhood to adulthood, her moral perspective is being formed as she acquires certain habits and skills and receives training in virtue. Yet it goes against central Christian convictions to claim that God loves humanity, that God befriends humanity, *because* of human virtue. Only because of God's free and unconditioned grace is humanity saved from its sin.

Such issues have led many Protestant exegetes and theologians to be nervous about describing Christian life through the use of language like "imitation of Christ," "friendship with God," and "virtues." Such language appears to detach the moral life from the objective accomplishment of human righteousness in Christ. It directs attention toward human action and away from the prior action of God. What is needed is a recognition that moral status is imputed to the ungodly; the justified sinner is first and foremost a passive recipient of righteousness and only subsequently a doer of good works. In Thurneysen's terse words, "Following Jesus never means imitating Jesus. Following Jesus always means coming under his fulfillment."[73]

Yet such fears are grounded in an unfortunate separation of person and works. Such a separation results in what Otto Weber calls "pneumatological docetism," by which he means a view "in which works would no longer be the work of a person, but an event independent of the person, so that they could be described but would never need to be the object of someone else's responsibility."[74] In short, the problem with such a separation—all too common in Protestant theology and ethics—is that the subject as an agent with duration through history is eliminated or at least paralyzed by the sole agency of Christ.

What is needed instead is a way of speaking of the prior action of God, namely the saving life, death, and resurrection of Jesus Christ, which also calls forth an account of the shape human activity is to take in response. Such an emphasis is found by recovering the relationship between being *conformed* to Christ and being called to imitate—or, as I think is preferable language, to *pattern one's life in*—Christ. God befriends humanity in Jesus Christ, and in that gracious action, which originates in God alone, humanity is conformed to Christ independently of particular characters, virtues, and actions. Grace is the fundamental orientation of Christian life. The context of this *conformitas Christi* is discovered in the salvation wrought by Christ; it is a salvation revealed throughout the context of his life, death, and resurrection.

It is worth recalling here the significance of the Lukan passage which identifies Jesus' salvation as connected particularly to those who are *not* (in the conventional sense) virtuous or in any way able to claim merit for their own activities; they are conformed to Christ because Christ befriends them. Moreover, the Johannine passage suggests, as does Thomas, that the significance of the cross can be seen in the context of friendship:

"Greater love has no man than this, that a man lay down his life for his friends" (John 15:13).

Yet because humanity has been conformed to Christ, people are also called and invited to a new way of life. If by grace humanity is conformed to Christ and brought into the mystery of the Triune God, through (in Thomas's language) charity people are to reflect that new life in discipleship. God's grace in Jesus Christ both enables and requires a life of virtuous discipleship. The life of discipleship is an achievement that comes by way of a gift. This appears in a particularly clear light in John 15. Following the connection made between friendship and the cross in 15:13, Jesus says: "You are my friends if you do what I command you" (John 15:14). Through Jesus' death in friendship the disciples are conformed to Christ, and they remain in Christ's friendship if, and insofar as, they follow his commandments and become friends to others.

Of course one way to read this passage is that if the disciples *do not* follow Jesus' commands, they will presumably become like the tax collectors and sinners to whom Jesus is friend in the synoptics.[75] I am not persuaded by such a strong reading of the Johannine passage, though there certainly are differences between John and the synoptics on this issue. The primary claim is that for those who have been befriended by Jesus, it is (theo)logically inconceivable—though practically conceivable and perhaps even likely—that they *would not* follow Jesus' commands. Even so, the objection is well taken insofar as it is a reminder that Jesus' friendship is open to all, regardless of what people do or who they are.

In the light of Jesus' friendship, the Christian's vocation, in response to God's prior action in Christ conforming humanity to his righteousness, is to pattern her life in Jesus Christ through discipleship. A person is called and enabled to pattern her life in Jesus Christ because God in Christ has patterned human life into God's life in order to save humanity. As I will indicate more fully in the next chapter, such practices as baptism, eucharist, forgiveness-reconciliation, and "performing" the Scriptures are indispensable practices whereby people learn to become disciples, whereby people learn to be friends of God and to befriend and be befriended by others. Through such practices, people are enabled to acquire the habits and skills reflective of the pattern discovered in Jesus Christ.

The second and closely related dimension that needs to be identified is the dialectical relationship between formation and transformation occasioned by conversion to a new way of life. Moral formation is necessary and indispensable to an account of moral judgment, and we are formed in and through particular friendships and particular practices. Yet Christianity is predicated not so much on the moral formation of the young as on the moral transformation of people who are converted to a new way of living.

On one level, an account of moral formation works as a description of what goes on *as a result of* conversion. It is important initially to recognize that conversion involves a fundamental reorientation of human life. In the recognition that God has befriended humanity which occasions conversion, people are convicted of their capacity for and the actuality of their evil, of the manifold ways in which their sin has prevented and continues to prevent them from growing morally because of their bondage to past distortions, deceptions, and rejections. It is only in seeing the truth about herself, brought about by God's grace, that a person can attain the true sorrow and forgiveness which constitutes her *metanoia*.

When God breaks into the reality of human life and shows the truth of what and who people are, healing takes place. God interrupts the continuity of life in order to heal and renew that life. As a consequence of such an interruption, becoming Christian requires a radical reorientation of one's life, a transformation of the self. As Rowan Williams puts it, "So to come to be 'in Christ', to belong with Jesus, involves a far-reaching reconstruction of one's humanity: a liberation from servile, distorted, destructive patterns in the past, a liberation from anxious dread of God's judgment, a new identity in a community of reciprocal love and complementary service, whose potential horizons are universal."[76]

Because conversion entails such a "far-reaching reconstruction," Christian language about conversion refers to being "born anew" (John 3:3) and becoming a "new creation" (2 Cor. 5:17). Such images suggest that life in some sense begins afresh at the point of conversion, at the point of the interruption of life where the Spirit begins to reconstruct a person's life in the light of Christ. Hence my account of the practice of friendship between parents and children is relevant to Christian life. The paradigmatic friendship for the Christian is between the parent who is God and the child who is the new convert; other such friendships derive analogically from this paradigm. Moral formation occurs as God interrupts a person's life, "befriending" her in that interruption so that she begins to learn—through practices wherein she acquires "praxological skills and virtues"— how she should live and what perspectives on the world she should have.

Hence on one level an account of moral formation such as can be found in Aristotle's *Nicomachean Ethics* can work by moving the context of habituation from an emphasis on the training of young children to a Christian focus on the training of "young" (whatever their biological age) converts. But while such a move is both conceivable and important for an account of Christian conversion and Christian life, the two perspectives are not so easily harmonized. While Christians can refer to the convert as being "born again" and hence beginning a new process of moral formation, and while it is true that the Spirit can start to work from anywhere, an Aristotelian will rightly insist that the new convert does not begin *de novo*. That is to say, she comes to Christianity as a person already habituated in certain perspectives; whatever else it is, the Christian context should not be described so much as moral formation as moral transformation. It is a *re*construction of humanity, a *re*orientation of moral perspective. And, the Aristotelians will suggest, the greater the divergence between the prior perspective and the Christian one, the more radical and difficult will be the task of reconstruction and reorientation; a person's habits, particularly ones that have become "second nature," are not easily broken or transformed.

Consequently on a second level Christians do have a stake in moral formation in an Aristotelian sense of habituation. This should not be assumed to be a formation centered upon an attempt to attain righteousness through works or human virtue; nor should it be taken to suggest that a person who is rightly formed will never need to be transformed. Rather the Christian stake in moral formation is centered in the belief that formation can help to render a person's transformations intelligible and desirable. As Oliver O'Donovan insists, "We shall not learn how to save our souls by talking about the formation of virtuous characters. Nevertheless, such talk may teach us better than anything else what it is for a soul to be lost or saved, and so teach us to care about it for ourselves and others."[77]

Moral formation occurs through an induction into the friendships and practices of Christian communities.[78] One dimension of Christian formation is to induct the young into the practices and friendships of Christian community such that, in the words of Horace Bushnell, "The child is to grow up a Christian, and never know himself as being otherwise."[79] It is a mistake to assume that persons *only* become Christian through emotional, datable, and dramatic conversions from a perspective radically different from Christianity.

However, even those who are raised within the Christian tradition are not immune from needing transformation, from needing to have their lives interrupted. At some point, every person must be "converted" in the sense that they must have their lives interrupted by God so that the continuity of their lives may be enhanced. Such conversions and interruptions may not, and in many cases will likely not, involve any dramatic or perhaps even datable events; even so, the claim is that all people are in need of being transformed so that they might become the persons God created them to be.

In addition, in all lives there are repeated occasions when people need to repent and to be transformed. Often the need for transformation occurs as the result of a breakdown of formation. Friendships and practices inevitably break down (the degrees to which they do so will vary) as the result of distortions and/or corruption such that persons are actually being malformed; hence reformation and transformation of relationships, practices, and people is an ongoing and never-ending task. But even when there is not a serious breakdown, there are always distortions and inadequacies in friendships and practices which require reformations and transformations of perspective.

An emphasis on moral formation provides the linguistic and moral resources which can render such transformations intelligible and desirable. Because humanity has been conformed to Christ, and consequently as people are enabled to become friends of God and others through lives of discipleship, they become better able to comprehend their capacity for evil, their destructive ways of ordering their lives, and the need for continual transformation. Put differently, the virtuous—

those whose lives have become ever greater reflections of the grace and friendship of God—experience their own sin and need for transformation in ways of which others are unaware. So it is through formation that the need for transformation becomes more sharply focused.

As there is a focus on transformation which nonetheless includes formation, so likewise the focus on formation necessarily includes transformation. The two stand in a complementary relationship and comprise essential components in an account of the shaping of Christian life and the activity of moral judgment.

The third dimension which needs briefly to be explored is the content of discipleship, and in particular whether there is one pattern to becoming a friend of God through discipleship or a plurality of paradigms. It is important to recognize initially that while Christian discipleship is shaped in the pattern of Christ, it needs to be construed in fully trinitarian terms. The gift of God's grace in befriending humanity through the life, death, and resurrection of Jesus Christ entails a response of friendship by becoming disciples, but that friendship-discipleship, which requires as one dimension befriending the neighbor, paradigmatically is an ever-deepening participation in the mystery of the Triune God.

When viewed in its wider context, the story of Jesus Christ reaches back to creation and forward to the consummation of the Kingdom. By being conformed to that story, people become part of the story of the Triune God. It requires that discipleship be construed along the lines of Nicholas Lash's "perichoretic dance" of Christian life, whereby the disciple recognizes the chaos, limits, and brokenness of life which reduces humanity to silence; is enabled to respond to the interruption of that chaos by the Word spoken, the life lived, and death undergone; and to participate in liberation and new possibilities through the power of creativity and transformation. The "dance of discipleship" derives its impetus and receives its decisive clarification from Jesus Christ, but it is nowhere appropriate to stop the dance and say "This is who God is, this is what discipleship means."

Thus a discipleship construed in relation to a trinitarian doctrine of God connotes that there is no one pattern to Christian life, no set description of how one must live if one is to become a friend of God. But a second question is important to ask, namely whether within trinitarian discipleship, in the patterning of one's life in Jesus Christ, there is only one pattern or a plurality of paradigms of how to live as disciples of Jesus Christ. John Webster appears to think there is only one pattern, grounded in a conviction that there is *one* story of Jesus Christ. So he repeatedly refers to *the* story of Christ, and *the* christological narrative.[80] But about such a claim three points need to be made.

First, there is, as has already been mentioned, an overarching narrative of Jesus Christ that is coterminous with the narrative of God's activity. It reaches back to creation and forward to the completion of the Kingdom.

Second, there is at least an outline of *the* story of Jesus Christ in relation to his life and ministry. It is readily assumed that Jesus of Nazareth lived, that he engaged in a public ministry for a period of time, that his ministry was marked by a concern for the disadvantaged in society, and that he was crucified under the reign of Pontius Pilate. However, beyond this outline, there is considerable variety both in how the outline is filled out and in the importance ascribed to those events for salvation and Christian discipleship.

Hence the third point is that Webster nowhere delineates what *the* story of Jesus Christ is, whether it is taken from one of the (presumably Gospel) writers of the New Testament or from a harmonization of their portraits. Indeed it is not clear even within the New Testament that Paul uses the "same" story of Jesus

Christ for all situations. As Stephen Fowl puts it, "Nor would it be adequate to claim that Paul has one large, coherent story which he applies differently in different situations, a sort of meta-gospel. Rather, the various stories of Christ Paul uses are, like his epistles in general, contingent interpretations of the traditions to which he is an heir, made in the light of specific situations."[81]

Thus within the New Testament there are diverse portraits of Jesus Christ, and there are also diverse patterns of discipleship patterned in Jesus Christ. Moreover, because in addition there is a manifold diversity of saintly lives which Christians have deemed to be reflections of Jesus Christ, there is a plurality of paradigms for discipleship. The diversity of saintly lives is crucial not only because of the inexhaustible significance of Jesus Christ, but also because such exemplars provide richly textured patterns for extending and revising the practices which are ingredient in Christian discipleship. From people as diverse in time, geography, and vocation as Melania the Younger, Ignatius of Loyola, John Wesley, Martin Luther King, Dorothy Day, and ordinary believers unknown to many by name but known by deed, Christians can perceive patterns of discipleship for their own lives and can also see patterns for reflective criticism of the current embodiments of friendships, practices, and understandings of discipleship.

The point needs to be made even stronger. The discipleship to which Christians are called, the task of becoming friends of God through lives patterned in Jesus Christ, not only offers a plurality of options dependent on contingent situations in which the believer finds herself; it demands the recognition that the patterning of life in Christ in particular, and discipleship construed in trinitarian terms in general, can only be complete in Christian community. The enactment of Christian discipleship is embedded in a shared way of life, and paradigmatic of this shared way of life is the communion of saints. As Karl Barth suggests,

> The saints of the New Testament exist only in plurality. Sanctity belongs to them, but only in their common life, not as individuals. In this plurality they are . . . identical with the Christian community. . . . The truth is that the holiness of the community, as of its individual constituents, is to be sought in that which happens to these men in common. . . . [82]

Hence friendship with God manifested in Christian discipleship is irreducibly a social phenomenon. People are incorporated into the friendships and practices of particular communities which shape people's discipleship, thereby recognizing that the patterning of life in Christ is only completed by the rich diversity which comprises Christian community.

The link between Christian life and the fulfillment of that life which is to be found in community should not be surprising, for ingredient in the Christian affirmation of God as Triune is a recognition of the centrality of Christian communities for the life of discipleship. If it is true that we *learn* to become persons by participating in the mystery of the Triune God, and if that learning takes its particular shape in friendship with God manifested in the practices of transformative discipleship, then it is important to explicate a bit more fully the practices of Christian communities and the pedagogies of Christian discipleship in which such moral formation and transformation occurs. Such is the focus of the third and final chapter.

3. LEARNING TO LIVE IN THE MYSTERY OF THE TRIUNE GOD

COMMUNAL PRACTICES AND PEDAGOGIES
OF DISCIPLESHIP

The moral life, when understood in terms of Christian life, receives its shape and pattern from God's Trinity. The vocation of the moral life is to learn to see and act rightly by participating in the mystery of the Triune God. "Persons," on this understanding, are not what humans initially, privately, and inwardly are, but are what humans may hope and must struggle to become through balancing in tension the complex factors and forces that constitute human life in the world. Human identity is continually both under threat and under construction, and it requires both an individual and a social struggle to eliminate that which destroys and to enhance that which builds.

Becoming a person also requires participating in the friendships and practices of Christian communities, and paradigmatically the practice of friendship with the Triune God, for it is in and through those friendships and practices that the "production of the personal" is given its specific shape. Christian life is inextricably tied to a responsive friendship with God manifested in transformative discipleship. But how is such friendship with God and such transformative discipleship enabled by participating in the practices of Christian community?

This chapter is divided into three sections. In the first

section, I briefly indicate the ways in which the doctrine of God's Trinity entails a specific understanding of the shape and pattern of Christian community. The task of becoming friends of the God who befriends humanity in Jesus Christ requires an ongoing communal process of questioning the claims of the world from the standpoint of the Gospel and the radically generative significance of Jesus Christ. Understood in trinitarian terms, the Holy Spirit is at work in such a communal process, guiding the community as it puzzles over its own as well as its individual members' existence and character.

In the second and third sections, I outline more precisely the contours of the Christian life that is transformed in and through particular friendships and practices in friendship with God. I argue that the friendships and practices involved in becoming a "friend of God" entail a (re)shaping of people so that they are enabled to perceive themselves and the world more accurately and are enabled to live more virtuously. In the second section, I sketch the relations between Christian practices and Christian community, and in the third section I explicate some of the central friendships and practices which contribute to the pedagogies of discipleship. Ultimately I argue that the Christian doctrine of the Triune God is intimately connected to the friendships and practices of Christian communities in and through which Christians receive their distinctive formation and transformation in moral judgment.

3.1 TRINITY AND COMMUNITY

Because discipleship is shaped in the pattern of Jesus Christ, it is to be expected that Christian practices and friendships should paradigmatically revolve around discerning the significance of Jesus of Nazareth and consequently how people should live in light of his life. As

Rowan Williams suggests, Jesus of Nazareth's "revelatory significance is apprehended by way of what it means to belong to the community whose character and limits he defines—not simply as 'founder' but as present head and partner in dialogue and relation."[1] It is in and through particular Christian communities that believers are to explore and discern the revelatory character of the life, death, and resurrection of Jesus of Nazareth.

To belong to such a community is to acknowledge that Jesus is Lord. As a consequence of such an acknowledgment, Christian community is shaped by the ongoing process of discerning what the Lordship of Jesus means for the definition and life of the community and the lives of its members. As Williams points out,[2] to belong to a community defined by Jesus Christ is, for example, to use certain kinds of language: about the meaning of resurrection, about power manifested in weakness, about sin and reconciliation, about sacraments, about what is seen in one who is hungry, sick, or in prison. It is to ask questions about the relationship between Jesus and Israel, about the continuities and discontinuities between the gathered people of God in Israel and the reconstitution of such communities by Jesus. It is to be involved in the active commendation of Jesus as the determinative focus of commitment for— in principle—any human being, to remember that the community exists for the eschatological reign of God, not itself. It is to be preoccupied in the structure of its social life with issues about the relative standing of rich and poor, about the structure of "insiders" and "outsiders," about the relations between men and women, about the ways in which leadership should be exercised and power regulated, about how hostility should be faced and disagreements resolved about appropriate and inappropriate contact with the "unbelieving" world.

The fact that addressing fundamental theological

questions, as well as learning to employ a distinctive vocabulary, are characteristic of Christian community is a reflection both of the radically generative significance of Jesus of Nazareth and the community's ongoing puzzlement about its own existence and character in witness to Jesus. In his book *Resurrection* Williams makes the point that:

> the Church is not the assembly of the disciples as a 'continuation' of Jesus, but the continuing group of those engaged in dialogue with Jesus, those compelled to renew again and again their confrontation with a person who judges and calls and recreates.[3]

The task of becoming friends of the God who befriends humanity in Jesus Christ is an ongoing communal process of discerning the significance of Jesus Christ for the shaping of Christian life.[4]

Hence the claim that Jesus Christ is the revelation of God means that his life, death, and resurrection must be capable of illumining any of the manifold circumstances, situations, and cultures in which people find themselves. As Williams puts it,

> For the event of Christ to be authentically revelatory, it must be capable of both 'fitting' and 'extending' any human circumstance; it must be re-presentable, and the form and character of its re-presentation are not necessarily describable in advance.[5]

Thus while Christian discipleship is patterned in Jesus Christ (i.e., "re-presenting" Christ in the variety of human circumstances), knowing how that pattern should be contextualized is not necessarily describable in advance nor is it guaranteed to be immediately and intuitively apparent.

The work of judgment and discernment about how Christians should live and what they should do as faithful disciples is a continual process, and it requires ongoing communal discussion and discernment. This discernment whereby Christians rediscover and re-present Christ is, in trinitarian perspective, what is meant by the illuminating or transforming operation of the Holy Spirit. As Ray Anderson puts it, "Even as the Spirit was active in the Incarnate Logos, making possible a genuine human response and participation in the divine life, the Spirit continues to act in this *form* by re-forming [humanity] into the form of Christ."[6]

But the work of the Holy Spirit, whether in relation to the other persons of the Trinity or in relation to the Church and the lives of persons, is often obscured. John Milbank has recently argued persuasively that recent Christian thought has failed genuinely to appropriate the work of the Holy Spirit.[7] He suggests that narratives of the role of the Spirit are thin and weak, and that typically no reconceiving of the relationship of God to the world is involved in thinking about Pentecost. He claims that "time and time again the Spirit is seen as more immanent, more economic, than the other two persons: a 'go-between God' whose redundant mediation only obscures the immediacy of the divine presence."[8]

In place of such views Milbank suggests that the Holy Spirit needs to be construed in terms of a "second difference." The focus of his argument is on the role of the Spirit in relation to the other persons of the Trinity, in which he argues that the Spirit proceeds from "paternal-filial difference" and is in the situation of being "a listener to a rhetorical plea of one upon behalf of the other. As the Father is not immediately available, the Spirit must listen to, judge and interpret the testimony of the Son. . . ."[9] Milbank's construal has important implications for understanding the role of the Spirit in a Christian construal of the communal discernment necessary for formation and transformation in, and the formation of, moral judgment.

Seen in the context of Milbank's analysis, the Holy

Spirit is the one who listens to, judges, and interprets the testimony of the Son as the Christian community seeks to discern how faithfully to re-present Christ. Thus the Church is, in Milbank's words, "poised between this Christological pole which is 'given', objectifying and organic, and a pneumatological pole which is subjective, interpersonal and always leading us to complete the work of shaping ourselves in the image of Christ."[10] That is to say, Christian life is poised between the work of Christ who, by befriending humanity, has *conformed* humanity to himself and the work of the Spirit who, by listening, judging, and interpreting the testimony of the Word, is leading Christians to become friends of God through discipleship in the pattern of Jesus Christ.

It may be objected that there need be no puzzlement about how Christians ought to live or what they ought to do; the Holy Spirit empowers the individual believer with the "fruit of the Spirit," and on that basis—and following the dictates and rules found in Scripture—the believer already knows how to live as a disciple. Hence, the objection would continue, my account of the Holy Spirit is too focused on the community; the Spirit works in the lives of individual believers, not in (a) community.

The second prong of the objection is not without merit, but it is more correct in what it asserts than in what it denies. It is true that the Spirit works in the lives of believers, but she does so through community, not independent of it. Paul's emphasis on the diversity of the Spirit's gifts (1 Cor. 12) reflects a vision of complementarity between the community's common life and the individual believer's particular embodiment of the pattern of Christ.[11] The Spirit is present in the concrete lives of other persons in the community, for it is in and through those other persons that the believer is enabled to see both that it is the whole community which is to approximate the complete patterning of life in Christ *and* that she represents an irreplaceable, non-transferable part of that pattern.

Thus the community reflects, in its diversity-in-unity, the image or likeness of the Triune God.[12] God "pours out" God's love into the community, giving concreteness to the intra-divine love.[13] Williams describes the trinitarian character of Christian community and its connection to the restoration and shape of Christian life with remarkable clarity: "In the resurrection community, the fellowship of the Spirit, the creative and sustaining power of God is shown to be identical with the compassion and forgiveness that renews and reconstitutes the relations of human beings with each other. 'God' appears in human history under the name of 'the one whom Jesus calls Abba'."[14]

Thus the second prong of the objection rests on an oversimplified understanding of the Spirit and the Spirit's relation to Christian life. What is needed is a more comprehensive trinitarian "grammar" of the relationship between personhood and community, a recognition that the doctrine of the Trinity constitutes the summary grammar for both discipleship and the life of the community.

The first prong of the objection, however, is predicated on an inadequate view of Christian life. The new life brought by Christ is not simply a canceling of the old; there is all the difference in the world, as Williams insists, between Christ uncrucified and Christ risen.[15] On the one hand, what is given by the risen Christ in the power of the Spirit is an interruption of people's lives that confronts them with the truth of what and who they are. Such an interruption enables people to own the stories of their past brokenness, self-deception, and complicity in evil. On the other hand, through that interruption the risen Christ also enhances the continuity of people's lives by giving them the *hope* that enables them to live into the future as faithful disciples.

Because Christian life involves a recovery of the past, not its obliteration, it is an ongoing task and struggle to discern how people should live and what they should do. Williams suggests that the truthfulness given to people, and sustained in them, by the Holy Spirit requires "a constant self-critical, alert, prayerful and receptive turning back to Jesus."[16] Because people must continually turn back to Jesus in order to discern the shape of Christian life, each depends on another—on the presence of another who, because of the particular configuration of her experiences, represents and embodies alternative understandings of the significance of Jesus. Community understood as friendship is thus crucial both because the otherness of the friend should serve as an interruption of a person's life and because the friend's life can enhance the person's understanding of the significance of Jesus.

Hence the objection fails. The Spirit is at work in the Christian community's puzzlement over its own as well as its individual members' existence and character.[17] For, as Williams suggests, "any such puzzlement over 'what the Church is meant to be' *is* the revelatory operation of God as 'Spirit' insofar as it keeps the Church engaged in the exploration of what its foundational events signify."[18]

That such is the case serves as a twofold reminder. First, it is a reminder that Christian life lived in the presence of the Triune God is inescapably eschatological; Christians are required to look toward a future that is not determined by humanity. Second, it is a reminder that Christian life cannot be wholly defined by rules. Puzzlement over what the generative significance of Jesus Christ implies for discipleship in diverse situations and contexts is typical rather than exceptional; thus any account which attempts to summarize and/or characterize Christian discipleship in terms of Kantian-like rules will be deficient. That is not to say, however, that rules have no place in Christian communities. As James William McClendon insists, "Where laws are understood as the rules for practices, and practices as the substance of an ongoing story, the necessity for their firmness and flexibility is alike evident."[19]

The shape of the community that continually seeks to discern how to live well in the midst of all the factors and forces of the world can be given further specification by Mikhail Bakhtin's account of polyphonic dialogue. Bakhtin rejects a "monologic" view of the world, the attempt to impose homogenization and unity, in favor of a "polyphonic" view which recognizes heterogeneity and diversity.[20] Such polyphonic dialogue entails the recognition that multiple voices need to be heard. Thus in Bakhtin's view we can only live and grow as we learn to listen to diverse voices and to engage in discourse with them. We do so not in the hope of gaining control over the voices, but for the purpose of engaging in joint inquiry.

Cast in theological terms, the community brought into being by God's Trinity exists without the ideal of a monologic unity. The community comes into being by the power of the Word, that self-utterance of God which gives voice to the silences of our complex and often fragmented lives and enables us also to hear others' silences as well as their voices. The polyphonic shape of Christian community entails an ongoing and open-ended process of dialogue, in which the Spirit guides and interprets our voices, about how we ought to pattern our lives in relation to the Triune God in the midst of the complexities of the world. The attempt to deny any feature of the world, whether it be creativity and joy (on the one hand) or the existence of tragedies and evils (on the other hand), is a reflection of a monologic perspective that seeks premature stability, closure, and unity. The polyphonic perspective involves the recognition that people's lives are to be shaped by the perichoretic dance of discipleship and a correlative willingness to participate in the dialogues of Christian community about what that discipleship entails.

Thus discipleship is an ongoing learning process that requires the transformation of human lives and the acquisition of "praxological skills and virtues." Such transformation occurs, and such skills and virtues are acquired, through induction into and participation in shared friendships and practices of Christian communities. These practices—of which the practice of friendship is of determinative significance—have as their central focus the unsurpassable significance of the life, death, and resurrection of Jesus of Nazareth, and are guided by the listening, judging, and interpretive work of the Holy Spirit.

The practices wherein discipleship is learned are inextricably linked to structures and patterns of friendships found in Christian communities, thus suggesting that an adequate understanding of the process of becoming friends of God requires attention to the character, shape, and limits of Christian communities and the friendships and practices which constitute such communities.

3.2 CHRISTIAN PRACTICES AND CHRISTIAN COMMUNITY

Since friendships and practices are important contexts for formation in moral judgment, and such practices are inextricably tied to particular communities and traditions, it is important to analyze the relationships among Christian practices, Christian communities, and the institutional infrastructures that are necessary for the ongoing practices of Christian community.

When discussing the kind(s) of Christian community effected by the Holy Spirit, it is necessary both to distin-

guish practices from institutions *and* to keep the relativ-
ity of the distinction in perspective. The practice of
Christian community (e.g., a forgiving-reconciling community of friends) is sustained by other practices (e.g.,
baptism, eucharist, interpretation and proclamation of
Scripture, feeding of the hungry) and is tied to institutional forms (e.g., structures determining the acquisition and distribution of power, status, and money)
which themselves may either fulfill their role by including and/or developing practices or deny that role by
remaining "mere" institutions which frustrate practices.
As Leonardo Boff argues, unity-within-diversity "can
be built up organically only in a community that is per-
petually renewing itself, overcoming the hardening of
its institutional arteries. It becomes 'the body of the
Three' not by merely existing as a church and calling
itself such, but through its continual efforts to become
a community of faith, celebration, and service."[21]

There is a close relationship between Christian communities and Christian practices. But that relationship
needs to be spelled out more carefully by attending to
what is meant by each of the two notions, for both
Christian community and Christian practices have poly-
valent meanings.[22]

In the previous section I discussed Christian community as a reality brought into being and sustained by the
Triune God. Viewed in terms of the narrative shape of
Scripture, such community originates in Israel's constitution as the people of God, is reconstituted by Jesus,
and is sustained and guided by the Holy Spirit.[23]
Throughout there is both continuity and discontinuity,
reflecting the history of people's particular practices
(specifically in this case the practice of *koinonia*) in their
relationship to God.

But there is a crucial ambiguity in the notion of Christian community, for it is (and has been) used to describe
a variety of ways of arranging social relationships.[24] I

want to delineate four contexts in which Christian community is instantiated and effected by the Holy Spirit: one broader than what is generally termed "the local congregation," the local congregation itself, and two of more restricted scope than the local congregation.

In its broadest sense, Christian community refers to the whole company of believers, the whole company of those who have responded to God's actions of befriending humanity by seeking to live as disciples in friendship with the Triune God. It includes the "assembly" of all Christians not yet assembled in one place, including both the living and the dead. Thus understood, Christian community encompasses the diverse and competing interpretations of Christianity and what it means to be in the Body of Christ; it is structurally similar to the notion of "the Christian tradition." At this level, the definitive understanding of Christian community is provided by the perfected communion of saints, toward whose destiny Christians are moving in their life of discipleship in friendship with God.

In its more usual sense, Christian community refers to the habitual assembly in a place for people to worship, generally referred to as the "local congregation." Such communities are (more or less) explicitly identified with a particular "denominational"[25] institutional structure and its concomitant view about how the narrative of the Christian tradition should be told. In these communities (at least paradigmatically) the sacraments are celebrated and the Word proclaimed. Moreover, the ritual gathering of these communities serves as the focal point for most people who identify themselves as believing Christians.

This assembly is also, however, the context of Christian community most closely tied to institutional structures. In principle, and often in reality, institutional structures serve to facilitate and enhance the development of various Christian practices. However such institutional structures, because they are concerned with goods which are both coveted and scarce (e.g., power, status, wealth), also have tremendous potential for corrupting practices and malforming people. Hence local congregations, because of their ties to institutional structures, are those Christian communities most likely to have well-developed practices *and also* to have those practices (including the practice of making and sustaining community) corrupted by institutions. Consequently they are also most likely to allow their practices (and consequently their people) to be accommodated to standards and realities antithetical to Christian convictions.[26]

There are two other contexts of Christian community more restricted in scope than either of the first two. The third context takes seriously the promise of Jesus that "where two or three are gathered in my name, there am I in the midst of them" (Matt. 18:20). In this context, Christian community describes the kinds of encounters in which persons engage in ongoing Christian practices outside institutional structures (including the making and sustaining of Christian community through Christian friendship), ranging from ongoing friendships between Christians not part of the same local congregation or even denomination to ongoing gatherings of groups of Christians for such purposes as Bible study, prayer, and conversations about matters requiring moral judgment.

The fourth context of Christian community characterizes those encounters in which people engage in Christian practices but on an occasional, rather than ongoing, basis. This would characterize such encounters as one-time retreats, special conferences, and deliberate gatherings (e.g., conventions, councils, world assemblies) for addressing specific issues. What separates the fourth from the third context is principally the occasional nature of the gatherings such that the friendships discovered there are likely to be less durable and hence less formative. So while much of what I will outline below is applicable to both the third and the fourth contexts, my attention will focus on the third as the more determinative context of Christian community.

The various forms of Christian community in this third context frequently are designed to provide reformation and renewal to the whole Christian community (context one) as well as particular local congregations (context two). This is so in at least two ways. First, because they are newer modes of the practice of community such that the institutions connected to them have not had as long to become moribund and/or oppressive to practices, such communities come closer to being themselves practices and (at least have greater potential for being) less accommodationist.

Second, precisely because they are less denominationally and institutionally defined, as well as less structured by habits and rituals, such communities present in principle the opportunities of breaking down false divisions while acknowledging true differences (e.g., across denominations when Catholics and Protestants engage in the common practice of reading Scripture). Moreover, they contribute to exposing and overcoming false identities (e.g., the encounters that take place across cultures which show how any one group's practices are affected by cultural and economic realities).

Some kinds of Christian community, particularly those that meet habitually and hence develop (at least incipient) institutional structures, may develop into Christian community understood in terms of the local congregation.[27] This can happen in ways ranging from inclusive acceptance by already-existing Christian institutions (e.g., the Roman Catholic acceptance of the Franciscans) to schismatic separation with fault typically lying on both sides (e.g., what happened between the Anglicans and the Methodists). That Christian community can change over time provides a twofold reminder: first, that the practice of making and sustaining Christian community, like other practices, has a history of growth and/or decay; and second, that the distinctions I have drawn between the contexts are not hard and fast, but rather should be seen as part of a continuum.

One central practice of Christian life is the making and sustaining of these various kinds of Christian community. In addition, however, there are a variety of Christian practices and ways of engaging in such practices, and such practices embody and entail diverse patterns of friendship. The variety is constituted in part by the fact that some communities sustain practices such as footwashing that others have given up. Moreover, even where the "same" practice such as the eucharist is at the center of two different communities (e.g., Eastern Orthodox and Disciples of Christ), their ways of engaging in that practice (e.g., the "high" liturgical, eschatological, and cosmological focus of the Orthodox and the "low" communal, table-fellowship focus of the Disciples) *may be* sufficiently divergent as to question whether or not they are in fact involved in the *same* practice.[28] This is not necessarily to suggest that either practice is wrong, for they may be seen to be mutually compatible and complementary ways of "practicing" eucharist; each practice is "essentially contested."[29] Regardless of the seriousness of the divergence, there are diverse ways of engaging even in those practices which "all" Christian communities take to be—in some manner—ingredient in their ongoing existence.[30]

These observations, if pushed to their logical conclusion, might render the notion of a single Christian tradition incoherent. In such a case, the most that could be said is that there are many diverse traditions which are in some ways strikingly similar and in others remarkably different. Three comments about such a possibility are in order. First, there may be times when people and/or communities, who heretofore characterized themselves as standing within the Christian tradition, define themselves and their practices in such a way that they are now best understood as constituting a rival and competing, even if in some ways overlapping, tradition (e.g., Mormons).

Second, the concept of tradition needs to be understood in a broad, rather than a narrow, context. The Christian tradition embodies continuities of conflict about the practices that constitute the tradition. It should neither surprise nor unduly trouble people to discover, then, that there is such a considerable variety of practices; but such variety need not, and must not, cause a lapse into a lazy pluralistic relativism.

Third, it is increasingly the case that—due to a variety of social and economic, geographical, and ecclesial circumstances—people engage in practices across (as well as within) ecclesially defined communities. Here a distinction between "institutionally bound" and "institutionally unbound" practices is helpful.[31] Some practices such as baptism are institutionally bound; that is to say, they are *only* genuine practices within the context of particular institutional structures such as are provided by ecclesial groupings (context two of Christian community described above). Other practices such as eucharist are paradigmatically bound to institutions (hence the strictures which surround the sacramental celebration), but are unbound in the sense that on particular occasions and in specific circumstances eucharist will be celebrated in institutionally unbound settings. And yet other practices such as forgiveness-reconciliation and the interpretation of Scripture are institutionally unbound; they are practices which are not inextricably tied to any existing institutional structures (thus able to flourish in contexts two, three, and four of Christian community).[32] The more that such practices are allowed to flourish, and are provided contexts in which to do so, the richer will be the conversation/argument about the goods that constitute the Christian tradition.

Christian practices, though intrinsically good, can become significantly disabled and corrupted by a variety
of factors. For example, such disabling and corrupting
influences include institutional hegemony, cultural and
economic influences that produce sexist, racist, or clas-
sist patterns, the lack of virtuous exemplars, and the
continuing existence of sin in the lives of the practi-
tioners. Whereas Christian friendships and practices are
intrinsically good because they receive their specification and clarification from the life, death, and resurrection of Jesus Christ, they can be disabled both by the
tragedies, evils, and sin which continue to persist and
by a failure to cope with changing social and historical
circumstances.

In such cases, people may find themselves—if the
situation calls for it—engaging in practices outside ongoing institutional structures.[33] Three different ways of
engaging in such practices need to be identified, for
they have significant implications for understanding the
relationships between practices, communities, institutions, and the Christian tradition.

First, people may engage in the "same" practice differently as a means of rehabilitating the distorted and
corrupted practice as it is being done elsewhere. Second, people may develop new practices which are *sui
generis*, designed to address historically contingent circumstances which (for whatever reasons) are not being
addressed. Third, people may develop new practices
that imply a rejection of the old ones; in such cases, if
the old practice is close to the heart of the Christian
tradition and a Christian account of God, and essential
to Christian life, such rejection may result in those people being now located outside not only the institution
but also the Christian tradition.

Thus practices develop and decline, new ones
emerge and old ones disappear. But there are some
practices which appear to be essential for the distinctive

formation and transformation in moral judgment which Christian life entails. They are practices in which a Christian learns discipleship in friendship with God and is confronted by the presence of other Christians in friendship; such practices provide the occasions for forming and transforming people in moral judgment. Thus it is to an exploration of four of these practices— baptism, eucharist, forgiveness-reconciliation, and interpreting Scripture—that I now turn.

3.3 CHRISTIAN PRACTICES AND PEDAGOGIES OF DISCIPLESHIP

While there are interpretive disagreements about the shape of these practices among Christians in general and diverse communities in particular,[34] I will prescind from these disagreements where possible, focusing on the logic that makes them central practices and their connection to pedagogies of discipleship in friendship with God.

Baptism, specifically baptism into Christ, is the means by which people are entered into the narrative of the Christian tradition and begin the formation and transformation of perspective which being Christian entails. By being incorporated into a particular community of friends people are set on the journey of becoming friends of God.[35] The journey may begin as an infant, when the individual is baptized and welcomed as an incipient member of the Christian community; such baptisms are reminders that God's grace, God's bestowal of friendship, precedes the ability to respond. Even so, infant baptism is predicated on the assumption (in our day, perhaps a questionable one) that the community will provide the social environment (i.e., practices) whereby the child will be raised such that she will eventually "own" the faith for herself and undergo a transformation of perspective. Alternatively, the journey may begin as a believer, when the individual is baptized and welcomed into a (often radically) new way of life. But in either case baptism is at once a sacramental act of the Church *and* an ongoing process of "living into your baptism," of becoming friends of God through discipleship.

Hence it is important to stress the connection between baptism and the new life which it entails, the relation between the symbol of new birth and the bestowal of a new identity in the community. This relation is central to Paul's letters, and it receives perhaps its paradigmatic formulation in Romans 6:1ff. According to Paul, those who have been baptized have entered into the community defined by whom or whatever they are baptized into; [36] thus to have been baptized into Christ, as Paul describes it in Romans 6:3, is to have entered into the community ruled and defined by Christ.

Paul goes on to specify that this is a baptism into Christ's death and resurrection. On this view, baptism is a training in dying—specifically to sin, to the old self—so that people may be brought to newness of life. By the grace of Jesus Christ people are set free from the history of their sin and evil, of their betrayals and from cycles of victimizer and victim such that they can bear to remember the past in hope for the future. The connection between the pattern of Christ and the discipleship of the believer is unmistakable; as Fowl describes it, "Christ's resurrection gives definition to the new age which began when Christ's death terminated the reign of sin. Analogously, the believer, who in baptism has entered into the community defined by Christ's defeat of sin, receives a new identity defined by the resurrected Christ (i.e., newness of life)."[37]

Thus Paul claims that the practice of baptism inducts those who are baptized into the shared practices of the community defined and ruled by the story of Christ's life, death, and resurrection. As Rowan Williams contends, "to be a disciple, to be with Jesus, is to be baptized: baptism is the way in which each person is made present to Jesus, the same process that Jesus described as 'immersion,' the process of self-forgetting that leads to the cross."[38] Baptism into the story of Christ is a trinitarian event because Christ's story can only be fully told, as the New Testament reveals, as the story of the Triune God.[39] It is significant to remember that baptism into Christ is by the Holy Spirit, and that the Church baptizes "in the name of the Father, Son, and Holy Spirit."

So it is that baptism is the practice which represents the inauguration of the Christian's friendship with the Triune God. To be baptized is to be given a new identity, to be located in a new tradition. As MacIntyre suggests, "I can only answer the question 'What am I to do?' if I can answer the prior question 'Of what story or stories do I find myself a part?'"[40] Quite profoundly baptism represents the changed context in which the Christian is now located;[41] no longer under the grasp of the false and self-deceptive traditions of sin, the Christian is defined by her incipient friendship with the Triune God.

In this context the twofold character of baptism is illumined. The individual is baptized only once, for the induction is a singular event that provides a new story and tradition which defines her life and gives her a new identity; however, the task of responding in "newness of life," the life of friendship with God through discipleship, is an ongoing process of "unlearning" the old identity and "learning" the new identity characterized as "living into her baptism."[42]

In the process of living into her baptism, the believer's life becomes a testimony to the risenness of Jesus. As Williams describes it, the believer "demon-

strates that Jesus is not dead by living a life in which
Jesus is the never-failing source of affirmation, challenge, enrichment and enlargement—a pattern, a
dance, intelligible *as* a pattern only when its pivot and
heart become manifest."[43] But manifesting the risen
Christ in one's life is not automatic; it is a difficult task
that requires an ongoing deconstruction and reconstruction of one's life in and through the community of the
Holy Spirit.

The tension between the new identity conferred in
baptism and the ongoing process of living into that baptism is given additional clarity by Kenneth Surin. Surin
suggests that at the point of being baptized the human
subject is suspended between two narratives, one "pre-
Christian" and the other "Christian"; she is thereby
poised to undergo a transformation. Surin draws on an
observation Fredric Jameson makes in a different context to describe the shape of that transformation. It is

> the shock of *entry* into narrative, which so often resem-
> bles the body's tentative immersion in an unfamiliar
> element, with all the subliminal anxieties of such sub-
> mersion: the half-articulated fear of what the surface of
> the liquid conceals; a sense of our vulnerability along
> with the archaic horror of impure contact with the un-
> clean; the anticipation of fatigue also, of the intellectual
> effort about to be demanded in the slow apprenticeship
> of unknown characters and their elaborate situations,
> as though, beneath the surface excitement of adventure
> promised, there persisted some deep ambivalence at the
> dawning sacrifice of the self to the narrative text.[44]

Surin suggests that the Church is the community which
enables the baptism to take place and to be lived
through.

Even so, Surin points out that while baptism inducts
the believer into the shared practices of the community,
locates her in a new tradition, and confers on her a new

identity, the individual still has been formed in "the ways of the world." As Surin describes it,

> this individual, member of the believing community though she may now be, is still a citizen of the world— she is *still* the modern, empty and deracinated subject. Conferring on her a new 'identity', even though that 'identity' may be one that is recognizably 'Christian', may in fact have the undesirable consequence of fixing and stabilizing this still empty subject.

Thus what is needed is a focus on what Julia Kristeva calls a "subject-in-process."[45]

Because the human subject is constituted by language, the ability to deconstruct the old identity and refashion a new life in Christ pivots on the possibility of discovering a disrupted and creative language that both deconstructs/demystifies and refashions through interrogation. So Surin suggests that "the church is the gospel-shaped 'narrative space' where Christians learn to sacrifice themselves, over and over again, to the community's narrative texts. This they do by consenting to be interrogated by these texts in such a way that they learn, slowly, laboriously and sometimes painfully, to live the way of Jesus."[46]

Surin's claim is that "living into your baptism" is a serious, ongoing, and difficult process. However, Surin's critique of the language of "identity," directed at such figures as Hans Frei and George Lindbeck, goes too far in denying what *is* in fact claimed about baptism. The task is not to focus *either* on the new identity conferred in baptism *or* on the "subject-in-process" that is the ongoing process of living into that baptism; rather it is to recognize the twofold character of the practice of baptism.

If baptism is the sacramental practice that initiates the journey of friendship with God, the eucharist is what provides sustenance along the way. I have already identified Thomas's understanding of the eucharist as the sacrament of friendship with God, the practice which preserves people from the sin that separates them from God and which provides the nourishment necessary for the journey toward perfect friendship with God.

In this context, then, I want to focus on two other dimensions to the practice of eucharist central to a Christian's transformation in moral judgment: first, it is a recollection of the story of Christ in the power of the Holy Spirit that entails both judgment and forgiveness; and second, it is an eschatological meal of friendship that recalls Jesus' table-fellowship and looks forward to the great Messianic banquet in the Kingdom and fellowship in the perfected communion of saints.

The eucharist, particularly in the narrative recollection of the Great Thanksgiving, is centered in a remembrance of Christ's saving sacrifice and a celebration of his continuing presence in the bread and the wine. As such, by participating in the practice of eucharist people are to pattern their lives in Christ by responding with an offering of themselves in Christ. Eucharistic practice provides the context whereby, as with baptism, believers are continually located in Jesus Christ by the power of the Holy Spirit. Being so located is the means whereby the recollection of Jesus Christ sustains people in friendship with God. As St. John Chrysostom puts it, "God does not need anything of ours, but we stand in need of all things from God. The thanksgiving itself adds nothing to God, but it brings us closer to God."[47]

However, as was the case with baptism, there is a twofold character to the practice of eucharist. The eucharist is a sacramental act of the Church in which people participate in praise and thanksgiving, and it also is an ongoing process of "eucharistic living." Christian life is to reflect the eucharistic sacrifice; Christ's pattern is not only to be observed, praised, and given thanks for in the liturgy, it is—by grace—to be entered into in the power of the Holy Spirit. Williams makes the point with characteristic clarity: "We are invited to grasp the truth that to eat at Jesus' table is to benefit from his total self-offering—in historical terms, from his death on the cross. Our redemption, our transformation, experienced as we find ourselves his guests, depends on nothing less."[48]

Such eucharistic living is an ongoing process because the transformation of the believer's old life (the "pre-Christian" narrative) into the new life (the "Christian" narrative) requires a continual dialectic of unlearning-deconstruction and relearning-formation. Hence it is important to remember that, as Paul writes to the Corinthian Church (1 Cor. 11:27–34), the eucharist is a vehicle of dominical judgment. Christ comes in the eucharist, and he comes both as Savior and as Judge. As Geoffrey Wainwright expresses it,

> The reason why the eucharist may turn into a condemnatory judgment is the fact that, despite our baptismal acceptance of the divine judgment on sin, we are still prone to sin. Nor, despite the forgiveness conferred on us sacramentally in our baptism, have we yet heard the final pronouncement of forgiveness at the last assize and entered to take our place at the meal of the kingdom. . . . [49]

In his earthly life Jesus enacted judgment within the relations of human beings to each other, and his judgment breaks the cycles of violence and sin because he forgives rather than condemns. When the risen Christ confronts humanity by the power of the Holy Spirit in the eucharist, however, Christians are reminded of, enabled to remember, their sin and betrayal of Christ's friendship because they have also experienced Christ's saving forgiveness and restoration of their lives.

A tragic estrangement and alienation exists between people, and between humanity and God, because people perpetuate cycles of violence and evil. In the eucharist the one who saves humanity from that estrangement and alienation comes as the one humanity made its enemy who, by grace, continues to be humanity's friend. People are enabled to recognize in the risen Christ the one who judges but does not condemn, who comes as a stranger who is yet also a friend.[50] Williams's description is significant: "The risen Jesus is strange and yet deeply familiar, a question to what we have known, loved and desired, and yet continuous with the friend we have known and loved."[51]

The process of so recognizing Jesus, and truly being set free from earlier identities in all of their destructive hold on people, is neither easily nor immediately achieved; it is a task in which Christians are continuously involved and enabled by the Holy Spirit in responsive friendship to God's grace in Jesus Christ. Seen in this light, the eucharist is a central practice wherein people are continually judged and forgiven, reminded that the gift received in which God befriends humanity in Jesus Christ carries with it the task of responding by becoming friends of God through lives of discipleship.

A second dimension of the eucharist that needs to be highlighted is its character as an eschatological meal that looks back toward Jesus' table-fellowship and looks forward to the perfected communion of saints. The fellowship at the Lord's table involves fellowship with one another; hence eucharistic practice is constitutive of a community of friends whose community is defined in no other way than by the parameters of the community Jesus invited to the table. It is an open invitation that breaks down the barriers of gender, race, class, education, nationality.[52] Moreover, as the community of Jesus' friends was sustained during his life by the sharing of food and drink and fellowship, so after the resurrection the community is sustained in the same way.

Table-fellowship was a central place where Jesus befriended the manifold diversity of humanity, and in particular those who are downtrodden, forsaken, and despised. So eucharistic practice is similarly structured, as those who gather at the table in responsive friendship with God extend that friendship by befriending others. In Williams's words, "the community of Jesus' friends is driven to enlarge and open itself, and this impulse is interpreted as God working as 'Spirit'."[53]

Friendship with God, which is both learned and expressed in eucharistic table-fellowship, involves the transformation of the believer's affections; those who before, and outside of the context of, friendship with God seemed unlovely and unlovable now appear lovable. Eucharistic friendship, then, is a practice in which Christians' friendship with God enables them increasingly to see in each and every individual—regardless of background or present circumstances—someone who is to be befriended.

The eucharist is not only a meal, however, that looks back to Jesus' table-fellowship; it is an eschatological meal that looks forward to the communion of the saints. In the eucharist Christians receive a foretaste of the great Messianic banquet, and its effect on their lives is profoundly trinitarian. Williams writes that the "attempt to live eucharistically, to transform our world into a community of gift, is more than merely obedience to a command, more than the imitation of a remembered historical pattern of life: it is the uncovering of the eternal *sapientia* of God."[54]

Thus the eschatological eucharist is the practice which links the friendship of the "developing" communion of saints in time with those in the *communio sanctorum*, the "perfected" communion of saints.[55] Pierre-Yves Emery describes the relationship well: "All that our friendship for those who go before us makes us say to God about them, finds its source, its perspectives and its bounds in the Eucharist. For it is in communion with Christ that we learn how the communion of saints is given life and expression."[56]

For it is the saints—in all of their diversity—who are the "patterns" whose lives re-present in new (and perhaps unpredictable) ways examples of the fullness of discipleship in friendship with God. The communion experienced in eucharist connects believers through the power of the Holy Spirit to the communion of the saints; as Robert Imbelli puts it, "The Spirit engenders in those who yield to her movement an absolute passion for communion; . . . the communion of saints is not only the communion the saints comprise, but, even more, the communion they effect."[57]

Thus it can be said that eucharistic practice is constitutive of friendship with the God whose saving events in Jesus Christ are recalled, recollected, and remembered through the narrative of the Great Thanksgiving and his presence in the bread and wine, and it is constitutive of friendship both with those who are in need of being befriended (recalling Jesus' table fellowship) and with those whose lives manifest—through a foretaste of the great Messianic banquet—something of the fullness of discipleship in friendship with God. The practice of eucharist brings to ritual focus life in relationship to God and to one another; and as a consequence of the friendship with God and with one another Christians enjoy at the table, they are—as an integral part of the practice of eucharist—to embody that friendship in a new way of life empowered by the Holy Spirit.

The two Christian practices of baptism and eucharist are central because of the role they play in the constitution and sustenance of Christian community and of individual believers' lives within the community. The practices are themselves formative and transformative of Christians' understandings of, and capacities for making, moral judgments. They entail the shaping and reshaping not only of the ways in which Christians think but also how they feel and how they act.

Moreover, both baptism and eucharist are practices that are determinatively trinitarian in character. Baptism is done in the name of the "Father, Son, and Holy Spirit," and the individual is baptized "into Christ" by the Holy Spirit. Likewise, in the eucharistic liturgy thanksgiving is offered for the gift of the Son's sacrifice in the power of the Holy Spirit, and following communion the believer prays in the power of the Holy Spirit that she may live a life of holiness in conformity to the pattern of Jesus Christ.

Both the trinitarian structure of these two practices and the role the practices play in the constitution and sustenance of community are important for understanding the character and shape of Christian community in its ongoing puzzlement about moral judgment, about how to live and what to do. The community structured around baptism and eucharist is a community brought into being by the Triune God, the reality who has made possible a particular way of living in community such that we may become persons.

Implicit in the description of the practices of baptism and eucharist, and more specifically in the characterization of the twofold shape of those practices, is an understanding of the importance of forgiveness in Christian life. That understanding needs to be made more explicit, for the practice of forgiveness-reconciliation is crucially tied to the making and sustaining of Christian community.

The forgiveness of sin is at the heart of the Christian gospel. Communities that come into being bearing the name of Christ are to be communities in which forgiveness, not punishment, is the norm. In the same way in which God has befriended and continues to befriend humanity, has reconciled and continues to reconcile humanity to Godself, through forgiveness rather than punishment, so Christian community is to be shaped in friendship by the same dynamic of forgiveness-reconciliation. This is brought to ritual focus in the individual's baptism unto the forgiveness of sin, and is to be embodied as the new believer lives into that baptism in newness of life. Moreover, the passing of the peace at the eucharist is a reminder that, as the eucharist recapitulates Christ's forgiveness of sin (Matt. 26:28), so also there is to be no enmity between those who come to eucharist (Matt. 5:21–26, 1 Cor. 11:27–29).

While the practice of forgiveness-reconciliation receives its ritual focus in the practices of baptism and eucharist, it is not confined to them. Indeed it is a practice that is necessary for the formation and sustenance of Christian community in all of its diverse contexts. It is an institutionally unbound practice, which is to say that wherever and whenever Christians are gathered together, forgiveness-reconciliation is to mark the shape of the community. Without such forgiveness-reconciliation, Christian communities would inevitably fracture and thus be unable to engage in the processes of discernment necessary for formation and transformation in, and of, moral judgment.[58]

Thus the dynamic of forgiveness-reconciliation is a crucial practice for the making and sustaining of Christian community, based upon and empowered by the forgiveness received from God in Jesus Christ (Eph. 4:32). McClendon summarizes the point well when he writes that it is the practice of "forgiveness that is the divine gift enabling disciple communities to cope with the looming power of their own practice of community, otherwise so oppressive, so centripetally destructive. Without forgiveness, the social power of a closed circle may crush its members, soil itself, and sour its social world. . . . But with forgiveness controlling everything, the closed circle is opened, the forgiven forgivers' practice of community is redeemed and becomes positively redemptive; thus this powerful practice renders obedience to the law of the Lord Jesus."[59]

The Christian communities centered upon the practices of baptism, eucharist, and forgiveness-reconciliation are the primary locus wherein Christians are formed and transformed in moral judgment and enabled to engage in patterns of discernment for the formation of moral judgments. These communities receive their shape, their patterns of formation and transformation, and their processes of discernment from the Triune God. The confession of these communities that it is *this* God, "Father, Son, and Holy Spirit," who enables the communities to exist and the practices of baptism, eucharist, and forgiveness-reconciliation to continue to form and transform both the community and the lives of believers, directs attention back to those texts which unfold in narrative form the Triune identity of the mystery of God.[60]

Hence Christian community and Christian life require as an ongoing task the practice of interpreting Scripture. Indeed it is in the process of being interrogated by the texts which Christians identify as Scripture that believers, under the guidance of the Holy Spirit and in a context of forgiveness-reconciliation, puzzle about how discipleship should be understood and, more importantly, lived. Such puzzlement is inevitable because the life, death, and resurrection of Jesus Christ does not yield a single univocal pattern of discipleship; Scripture itself is a diverse, multi-stranded witness to the Triune God and yields a diversity of patterns of discipleship.[61] Such puzzlement entails thinking analogically from the various contexts of Scripture to the various contexts in which believers find themselves in the world.

Such puzzlement also arises because of the ways in which people do not "see" rightly. To say that Scripture "creates" a world,[62] or that Scripture "creates" the community as the bearer of a world,[63] is in one sense quite accurate but in another quite misleading. Becoming a Christian involves learning to live in a "new" world; so in that sense it is an accurate claim. But Scripture does not "create" anything *de novo;* in the encounter with biblical texts believers' "old" selves and perceptions of reality are confronted with that new world. Hence the emphasis must be placed on *learning* to live in that world, for as I suggested in my discussion of baptism, that learning requires as a necessary correlative a rather extensive deconstruction (an "unlearning") of all the ways in which people's perception has been distorted such that they are unable to see the world for what it is. Hence a Christian community faces ongoing puzzlement in its encounters with Scripture because accurate and appropriate discernment is a task which must be achieved; it cannot be assumed, nor is it simply "created."

In communities Christians learn—as the body of Christ by the power of the Holy Spirit—to interpret, and to have their lives interrogated by, the biblical texts such that they are formed *in* the kinds of moral judgment necessary for them to live faithfully as friends of God. Christian community is best understood as a community of friends. Integral to the friendship which Christians share (derived from their friendship with God) is a conversation in which their mutually reciprocal pedagogies are designed to deconstruct all that which prevents people from seeing rightly and living well—that which they, prior to their "conversion" to a new life, understood to comprise "reality"—and thereby also to liberate them for an ever-deepening discipleship in friendship with God. Christian communities are the occasions in which, in the context of the "dangerous" remembrance of Christ's passion, believers are enabled by Christ's resurrection to converse about how faithfully to live as friends of God. Williams describes the link between the resurrection and Christian conversation about how lives should be shaped: "The resurrection of Jesus, in being a restoration of the world's wholeness, is equally a restoration of language; what is created in the community of the resurrection is not only a vision of humanity before God and with God, but a vision capable of being articulated in word and image, communicated, debated, and extended."[64]

Thus communal discernment—the conversation in the good which is both formative and transformative and involves both deconstruction and construction of identities—entails a polyphonic dialogue that is enabled by the Holy Spirit through Christ's resurrection, and involves an ongoing task of interpreting Scripture which requires for its achievement the acquisition of a range of "praxological skills and virtues" by the members of the community. Such skills and virtues are given their shape and form through irreducibly diverse lives of discipleship in friendship with God, and they are learned in and through particular practices. Through these practices believers are habituated in (particular kinds of) virtue. While I cannot here characterize or defend a table of Christian virtues, I would suggest that central Christian virtues would include charity, hope, faith, patience, peaceableness, perseverance, remembrance, righteousness, cruciformity,[65] "obedient suffering,"[66] and the dynamic of forgiveness-reconciliation. There is no way to configure the virtues in the abstract, nor is it possible to guarantee in advance what kinds of behaviors they entail. Such virtues receive their specification in and through the particular contexts in which believers find themselves.

In general, however, they are virtues that enable praxis, that show forth a witness to God's ways with the world. They are exemplified in lives of discipleship which can be described, in Nicholas Lash's suggestive image, as "performing the Scriptures."[67] The interrogation which people undergo in their conversation with

Scripture has as its *telos* a performance of Scripture. Lash puts it as follows:

> Christian practice, as interpretative action, consists in the *performance* of texts which are construed as 'rendering,' bearing witness to, one whose words and deeds, discourse and suffering, 'rendered' the truth of God in human history. The performance of the New Testament enacts the conviction that these texts are most appropriately read as the story of Jesus, the story of everyone else, and the story of God.[68]

What Lash is suggesting is that, as the fundamental form of the interpretation of one of Beethoven's late string quartets or the interpretation of Shakespeare's *King Lear* is the performance of the texts, so the fundamental form of the interpretation of Scripture consists in its performance.

There is an important disanalogy. While *King Lear* or Beethoven may involve performance as the *telos* of the texts, they do not structure or shape the performer's life. Yet that is precisely the claim that Scripture makes on a Christian's life. One can perform Shakespeare masterfully for a couple of months and then move on to performing Arthur Miller or Neil Simon, or alternatively one can perform Shakespeare masterfully while failing to embody in one's other activities a Shakespearean pattern of life; however one cannot perform Scripture adequately, let alone masterfully, unless it structures and shapes the entirety of one's existence.

With this disanalogy in mind, Lash's image is significant because it illuminates the practice of interpreting Scripture in Christian community. Lash suggests that Christian living, construed as the performance of Scripture is, for two reasons, necessarily a collaborative enterprise.[69] The first reason is that the performers need the help of "experts." Such experts include scholars who investigate the written texts as well as theologians who critically reflect on Christian practices, analyzing the performances and suggesting ways in which those performances can be improved.[70]

The second reason, Lash contends, arises from the nature of the texts: it takes two to tango and rather more to perform *King Lear*. Put in Christian terms, the full performance of Christian discipleship—which will only be achieved eschatologically—requires the whole company of humanity. But even now, in this time between the times, the performance of Scripture requires the entire Christian community (understood in its widest sense). Christian Scripture is performed and enacted as the social existence of the entire community; Christian discipleship is not complete as individuals, for it is the whole community whose life is to represent the complete discipleship in the pattern of Jesus Christ. As Lash describes it, "The fundamental form of the Christian interpretation of scripture is the life, activity, and organization of the believing community. The performance of scripture *is* the life of the church."[71] In this sense, then, while baptism, eucharist, and forgiveness-reconciliation direct people back to the texts of Scripture, Scripture also directs them to baptism, eucharist, forgiveness-reconciliation, and other practices of Christian community.

The practice of performing the Scriptures is intimately related to the practices of baptism and eucharist in another way as well. Performances vary both in breadth and in depth. The newly baptized member of the community will likely have a narrower range of options and a more superficial grasp of the texts; she lacks the requisite skills and virtues necessary for masterful performance. Here she will be guided by others in the community whose praxological skills and virtues are more varied, developed, and habituated.

That is to say, the interpretation of Scripture which has its *telos* in the performance of discipleship requires the development of virtues which enable that performance. In more Aristotelian terms, it involves the acquisition of *phronesis* by the community as well as its individual members.[72] The community possesses a shared *phronesis*, which involves a "thinking in common" under the guidance of the Spirit about how to relate the biblical texts to the particular material realities, cultural conditions, and concrete situations in which people find themselves.[73] Moreover, Christian communities (understood in each of the contexts) rely on exemplars to guide the newly initiated in making the link between discernment and performance; thus while there is a shared *phronesis* in interpreting Scripture communally, the interpretation of Scripture has as an indispensable and ongoing task forming and transforming persons in moral judgment so that the shared communal discernment may continually be deepened and the performances improved.[74]

Preeminently, however, the newly baptized Christian's paradigm for those who can guide her in Christian life will be those who are in the "perfected communion of saints." Here the eschatological dimension of the eucharist provides the connection linking believers with the perfected saints. The performances of the saints are paradigmatic because they represent the greatest range and depth of praxological skills and virtues, the most complete representations of the hermeneutical virtue of *phronesis*. In the performances of their lives, believers encounter different ways of embodying friendship with the Triune God. As Surin describes it, "The perfected *communio sanctorum* has a crucial regulative role to play in the process of helping all Christians to acquire the requisite skills for understanding the textual world created by the biblical narrative. The saints are the true interpreters of Scripture."[75] The saints are paradigms for Christian life, both personally and corporately, not because of who they are in themselves but because of the Triune God to whom the pattern of their lives bear witness.

Put in Aristotelian terms, the saints are paradigmatic for the performance of Scripture because their lives are indispensable "patterns" in whose apprenticeship people learn and acquire skills and virtues such that their performances will become increasingly less inadequate. Under the guidance of the saints people's lives and their judgments become—slowly, laboriously, and often painfully to be sure—ever-increasing reflections of the glory of the God who is humanity's friend. Imbelli describes the point vividly: "The Spirit of Christ narrates Christ's story in the lives of the saints, a narrative that is ever ancient and ever new; allowing us to be ravished once again by Christ's beauty, as it is embodied in the living text who is the saint."[76]

Thus the practice of interpreting Scripture, like baptism and eucharist, has a twofold character. On the one hand, it involves being interrogated by Scripture in community so that people's distorted vision can be restored and they can be liberated for lives of discipleship in friendship with God. On the other hand, it requires embodying that discipleship through performances of Scripture, performances in which Christians serve as apprentices under the guidance of friends within communities but paradigmatically under the guidance of the saints.

People become friends of God by responding to God's befriending of humanity through participating in the friendships and practices of Christian community. While people can certainly continue to participate in other practices seen to be compatible and/or convergent with the practices of Christian community, discipleship involves an "unlearning" of those practices which are part of traditions incompatible with Christianity. In this sense Christian practices constitute "counter-practices" to the prior practices of which the people were a part.

In particular, baptism, eucharist, forgiveness-reconciliation, and the interpretation of Scripture are central practices which form and transform human life such that believers are increasingly able to discern how they should live and what they should do. Such practices encourage the development of critical reflective thought among people. Such critical reflection is geared not only toward seeing and describing actions, the world, and our lives more accurately and less deceptively, but also toward the continual reformation and transformation of the friendships and practices of Christian communities as they are currently embodied.

Christian life entails a distinctive formation and transformation in moral judgment because that living is inextricably tied to responsive friendship with the Triune God and is enabled by participating in such central practices of community as baptism, eucharist, forgiveness-reconciliation, and the interpretation of Scripture. Christian living receives its "summary" grammar in the doctrine of the Trinity such that the pedagogies of Christian discipleship are (1) fundamentally shaped by communal friendships and practices, and (2) are directed toward an ever-deepening friendship with the God who befriends humanity in Jesus Christ and who enables responsive friendship through the power of the Holy Spirit.

Through formation, and more determinatively transformation, in the Christian tradition people learn to describe themselves, their actions, and the world. A Christian account of formation and transformation in moral judgment is grounded in the shared friendships and practices of Christian communities which have an ongoing puzzlement—a puzzlement in which the Holy Spirit serves as listener, judge, and interpreter—about how Christians should live and what judgments they should make in light of God's presence in, among, and for humanity in Jesus Christ.

Such a puzzlement is a reminder that, though Christian life receives its clarification and specification in the new order brought by Jesus of Nazareth, the old order persists. Hence in the perichoretic dance of discipleship it is important to balance in tension the various factors and forces that constitute human life in the world. No rigid barrier should be erected between the Church and the world. Even when Christian communities stand against the destructiveness of the world, they must do so for the sake of the world which is and remains God's good creation. The crucial issue involves discerning how, from the standpoint of the friendships and practices of Christian communities necessary to unlearn destructive patterns of feeling, thinking, and acting and to learn new ones, Christian communities and believers should serve in the world. Whether the issue involves, for example, the possible legitimation and/or tragic acceptance of the necessity of violence or discerning the limits and possibilities of appropriate vocations, discerning how to live in the mystery of the Triune God involves an ongoing puzzlement. Such discernment requires the practical wisdom gained in and through the formation and transformation of people's lives, and it is embodied in the polyphonic dialogues and shared lives of Christian communities.

Central to Christian convictions, then, is the belief that it is an exceedingly difficult task to see and describe the world rightly and to learn to think, feel, and act well. Indeed it is simply not possible to accomplish such a task except for the prior gracious activity of the Triune God who befriends humanity and enables people (through particular friendships and practices) slowly, laboriously, and painfully to unlearn destructive and self-deceptive views of the world and their lives in order then to learn the way of Jesus Christ and to live in the mystery of the Triune God. It involves people in the perichoretic dance of discipleship, a dance which includes discerning the pattern of one's life in Jesus Christ and puzzling with others about how that pattern is to be lived in specific historical and cultural contexts through the power of the Holy Spirit, and questioning the claims made by the world in the face of the transcendence of God. It is a dance in which believers can never stop as they continually seek to behold the glory of, and participate in, the mystery of the Triune God.

CONCLUSION

ENDING WITH A BEGINNING:
GOD, MORAL JUDGMENT,
AND MODERN SOCIETIES

I have argued that the activity of moral judgment is inextricably tied to a person's character and that such character is formed and transformed in and through the friendships and practices of theologically specified traditions. Through an exposition that connects the Christian depiction of God as Triune to a distinctive account of moral judgment, I have contended that views about such matters as God, the world, and life and death have a significant impact on the shape of formation and transformation *in* moral judgment and hence also the formation *of* moral judgments. In particular, I have suggested that the primary friendship a person should have is with the God who has befriended humanity in Jesus Christ, and that such friendship calls forth a life of transformative discipleship. Such discipleship is learned in and through the practices and friendships of Christian communities, which are given their shape and form by the mystery of the Triune God.

Many issues have arisen in the context of this book to which I have not given adequate attention. For example, while the activity of moral judgment has been important to the structure of the argument, the primary focus has been on the formation and transformation in moral judgment which is necessary for the activity of moral judgment. I have not attempted to provide a full account of the activity of making moral judgments, either methodologically or with reference to any specific issues. In order to have done so I would have needed to attend in more detail to such issues as the place of rules, the connection between moral judgment and accounts of practical reasoning, and the relationship between moral judgment and other kinds of judgments.

In addition, I have not sketched the possibilities for, or the limitations of, conversation across traditions with divergent theological, antitheological, or atheological views. Although people who appeal for "public" conversation about moral issues frequently fail to recognize the traditioned context of those appeals, it is not the case that people are prisoners in their traditions. The fact that traditions overlap in significant ways makes conversation about matters that matter possible; the fact that traditions diverge makes such conversation necessary.

A closely related issue is the fear that my argument for the centrality of traditions entails an anti-realism and/or a vicious relativism, though in fact it entails neither. To have taken up these questions, and in particular to have displayed how traditions can be subjected to rational comparison along the lines I think is possible, would have required a very different kind of book. If my argument helps to illuminate why such rational comparisons between and among traditions are necessary for moral inquiry, discussion, and debate, that will be a start.

I have not attempted to defend the Christian doctrine of God as Triune against challenges either from people outside the Christian tradition, as would come from a member of another religious tradition or from an atheist, or from within the Christian tradition, as would come from some "process" theologians or perhaps from "theocentric" ethicists. While there are avenues for response to both sorts of challenges, to have taken up those issues would have required a more detailed analysis of and comparison with rival traditions and accounts. That is an important and necessary pursuit for theological ethicists, but not one that I could take up here.

Such issues are important and are in need of further exploration, explication, and defense. But there is a different set of issues that have arisen in this book which are quite pressing. The issues center upon the relationship between God, theologically specified traditions, and modern societies. If people are to be able consistently to make wise moral judgments, to be people of character, we need to recognize that such character is formed in and through the friendships and practices of particular traditions. But what I have not shown is that the friendships and practices are feasible or meaningful in modern societies. One of the issues to be faced is whether or not goods external to practices (e.g., money, power) have become so dominant and determinative in modern societies that they have overwhelmed the goods internal to practices and brought those practices into significant if not complete disrepair.

But that is to put the issue still too optimistically. For if the practices are just in disrepair, then what is needed is some kind of corrective surgery to make them practicable again. The stronger challenge is whether certain features of modern societies—such as technologies, bureaucracies, and other modern economic structures—have become so dominant and powerful that it is exclusively them, and not traditions, which are producing the "characters" of modern societies.[1] After all, even with reference to the practice of friendship with God, the possibility of such friendship may be undermined *on our side* by a consumer mentality. As Martin Buber has suggested, "whoever knows the world as something to be utilized knows God the same way."[2]

If, then, theologically specified traditions require particular kinds of social contexts—those provided by any tradition's account of friendships and practices—in order to be sustained, what is needed are close analyses of whether and to what extent modern societies currently allow such social contexts to flourish. If not, or to the extent that they do not, what is also needed is careful criticisms of those patterns of modern societies which are destructive of friendships and practices and, hence, also moral judgment. This crucial matter involves not only whether, and how, people can engage in friendships and practices but also whether and how people can live in relation with the living God.

The perspective of this book suggests not only that such attention to, and criticism of, social contexts and their relation to modern societies and theological matters is necessary, but that in so doing a person will be arguing from within a tradition's account of the good and from that tradition's conception of what social contexts are necessary and/or desirable. Because there are diverse and competing traditions and hence diverse and competing accounts of wise moral judgment, there will be competing diagnoses of the problems of modern societies as well as competing prognoses for a cure.

It is impossible adequately to diagnose the problems of modern societies and to offer prescriptions for a cure without a particular vision of the friendships and practices people need to flourish. As Aristotle suggested at the end of his *Nicomachean Ethics*, accounts of ethics and moral judgment are closely related to accounts of economics and politics—to which I would add an account of theology. The interrelationship of these issues at once clarifies the task and makes its accomplishment more difficult; but I am convinced that there is no other way forward.

NOTES

Introduction

1. Edmund Pincoffs, *Quandaries and Virtues* (Lawrence, Kan.: University Press of Kansas, 1986), 4.
2. Ibid., 6.
3. Ibid., 7.
4. Ibid.
5. Ibid., 162.
6. Alasdair MacIntyre, *"Sophrosune:* How a Virtue Can Become Socially Disruptive," in *Midwest Studies in Philosophy 13, Ethical Theory: Character and Virtue,* ed. Peter A. French, Theodore E. Uehling, and Howard K. Wettstein (Notre Dame, Ind.: University of Notre Dame Press, 1988), 7.
7. Ibid., 6.
8. Pincoffs, *Quandaries and Virtues,* 91–92.
9. Martha Nussbaum, *The Fragility of Goodness* (Cambridge: Cambridge University Press, 1986), 4. She also notes differences between Greek Olympian religion and (what she mistakenly and oddly characterizes as) the God of the Judeo-Christian tradition. See her note 3 on 425–426.
10. Martha Nussbaum, "Narrative Emotions: Beckett's Genealogy of Love," *Ethics* 98 (1988): 225–254, reprinted in Stanley Hauerwas and L. Gregory Jones, eds., *Why Narrative?* (Grand Rapids, Mich.: Wm. B. Eerdmans, 1989): 216–248.
11. Martha C. Nussbaum, "Non-Relative Virtues: An Aristotelian Approach," in *Midwest Studies in Philosophy 13, Ethical Theory: Character and Virtue,* 38.
12. Ibid., 45.
13. Ibid., 33.
14. Ibid., 36.
15. Ibid., 39.
16. Ibid., 33.

17. Ibid., 34, 45 (emphasis added).

18. Ibid., 33.

19. Ibid., 46.

20. Ibid., 47 (original emphasis).

21. Though it is worth noting that her list is extremely problematic for a variety of reasons (e.g., the severely mentally retarded are at best marginal human beings given her claims about cognitive capacity and practical reason). Even her claim that humans die is problematic, as can be seen in such examples as the apostle Paul's conviction that the only morally significant death is the death to sin or a Hindu's conviction that beyond death there is reincarnation.

22. Nussbaum, "Non-Relative Virtues," 44.

23. Stanley Hauerwas, *Character and the Christian Life* (San Antonio, Texas: Trinity University Press, 1974, 3rd Printing 1985), 228.

24. Ibid., 227.

25. Stanley Hauerwas, *A Community of Character* (Notre Dame, Ind.: University of Notre Dame Press, 1981), 111–128.

26. Ibid., 129–152.

27. See the essays "Jesus: The Story of the Kingdom," and "The Moral Authority of Scripture: The Politics and Ethics of Remembering," in *A Community of Character*, 36–52 and 53–71.

28. Stanley Hauerwas, *The Peaceable Kingdom: A Primer in Christian Ethics* (Notre Dame, Ind.: University of Notre Dame Press, 1983).

29. It should be noted that Hauerwas moves in that direction in his essay "The Church as God's New Language," in *Scriptural Authority and Narrative Interpretation*, ed. Garrett Green (Philadelphia: Fortress Press, 1987), 179–198. The account there is suggestive but remains too sketchy.

1. Learning to Describe Actions, Persons, and the World

1. For an interesting discussion of the fact-value distinction, and of Hare's and Foot's positions about it, see D. Z. Phillips and H.O. Mounce, *Moral Practices* (New York: Schocken Books, 1970).

2. Pincoffs, *Quandaries and Virtues*, 162.

3. J. Philip Wogaman, "Review of *Character and the Christian Life*," *Religion in Life* 24 (1975): 382–383.

4. J. Philip Wogaman, *A Christian Method of Moral Judgment* (Philadelphia: Westminster Press, 1976), ix-x.

5. In the new edition of his book, unfortunately published after I completed this manuscript, Wogaman adds a short chapter on "Christian Character and the Virtuous Life." Even there, however, he fails to recognize the controversial status of descriptions. J. Philip Wogaman, *Christian Moral Judgment* (Louisville, Ky.: Westminster/John Knox Press, 1989), 27–38.

6. Charles Taylor, *Human Agency and Language: Philosophical Papers I* (Cambridge: Cambridge University Press, 1985), 4.

7. Clark L. Hull, *Principles of Behavior* (New York: Appleton-Century, 1943), 25–26.

8. Charles Taylor, *The Explanation of Behavior* (New York: Humanities Press, 1964).

9. Taylor, *Human Agency and Language*, 78.

10. Gilbert Ryle, *The Concept of Mind* (Harmondsworth: Penguin Books, 1963).

11. Barry Schwartz, *The Battle for Human Nature* (New York: W. W. Norton, 1986), 32.

12. Clifford Geertz, *New York Review of Books*, 24 January 1980, 4; cited in Schwartz, *Battle for Human Nature*, 325.

13. Taylor, *Human Agency and Language*, 78.

14. G. E. M. Anscombe, *Intention* (Ithaca, N.Y.: Cornell University Press, 1957), 9. Anscombe goes on to specify what constitutes a reason for acting, and she develops several distinctions which I will not attend to here. A full development of the notion of intention would require (1) an analysis of what it means to do something unintentionally, (2) a description of the relationship between intention and observational/non-observational kinds of knowledge, (3) an account of the relationship of present intention to future action, and (4) making a distinction between doing something "intentionally" and "by accident or mistake." There is an extensive literature on these questions. For examples of accounts that treat such questions, see, in addition to Anscombe, Stuart Hampshire, *Thought and Action* (New York: Viking, 1960).

15. Alasdair MacIntyre, "Ideology, Social Science, and Revolution," *Comparative Politics* 5 (1973): 323–324.

16. Eric D'Arcy, *Human Acts* (Oxford: Oxford University Press, 1963), 11–12.

17. Alasdair MacIntyre, "Praxis and Action," *Review of Metaphysics* 25 (1972): 740.

18. Herbert Fingarette, *Self-Deception* (New York: Humanities Press, 1969). For a use of Fingarette's analysis in a specific case, see Stanley Hauerwas and David Burrell, "Self-Deception and Autobiography: Reflections on Speer's *Inside the Third Reich*," in Stanley Hauerwas, *Truthfulness and Tragedy* (Notre Dame, Ind.: University of Notre Dame Press, 1977), 82–98.

19. Taylor, *Human Agency and Language*, 79.

20. Taylor, *Explanation of Behavior*, 58.

21. Charles Landesman, "The New Dualism in the Philosophy of Mind," *Review of Metaphysics* 19 (1965): 329–345; Richard J. Bernstein, *Praxis and Action* (Philadelphia: University of Pennsylvania Press, 1971), 278–299.

22. Bernstein, *Praxis and Action*, 279.

23. I say "at times" because at various points he qualifies the dualism, even though he does not overcome it.

24. Hauerwas, *Character and the Christian Life* (San Antonio, Texas: Trinity University Press, 1975), 95–96. The internal quotation is from John MacMurray, *The Self as Agent* (London: Faber and Faber, 1957), 160.

25. Alasdair MacIntyre, "The Intelligibility of Action," in *Rationality, Relativism, and the Human Sciences*, ed. J. Margolis, M. Krausz, and R. M. Burian (Dordrecht: Martinus Nijhoff, 1986), 63–80.

26. Alasdair MacIntyre, *After Virtue*, 2d ed. (Notre Dame, Ind.: University of Notre Dame Press, 1984), 208.

27. Ibid., 209.

28. Ibid., 211.

29. Ibid., 211–212.

30. Ibid., 216.

31. Ibid., 217.

32. Ibid., 218.

33. Ibid., 213.

34. Of course one of the problems with such "conversa-

tions" is the way in which power relations prevent both conversants from being "equal" partners. Though I cannot attend to such important issues here, the writings of Michel Foucault and Juergen Habermas are—in different and sometimes conflicting ways—important in this regard.

35. Richard Shusterman has recently argued for the importance of narrative in construing human life, and his suggestion that it will be a complex narrative entailing "unity in variety" cries out for the kind of trinitarian perspective I develop in the second and third chapters. See his "Postmodernist Aestheticism: A New Moral Philosophy?" *Theory, Culture, and Society* 5 (1988): 337–355.

36. MacIntyre, *After Virtue*, 216.

37. Ibid., 215–216.

38. Ibid., 219.

39. Ibid.

40. See, for example, Oliver O'Donovan, *Resurrection and Moral Order* (Grand Rapids, Mich.: Wm. B. Eerdmans, 1986), 221–222; J. Budziszewski, *The Resurrection of Nature* (Ithaca, N.Y.: Cornell University Press, 1986), 106.

41. I derive this interpretation of MacIntyre in part from an essay where he clearly defends a version of realism within a teleological framework. See his "Objectivity in Morality and Objectivity in Science," in *Morals, Science, and Sociality*, ed. H. Tristram Engelhardt, Jr., and Daniel Callahan (New York: Hastings Center, 1978), 21–39.

42. The content of the *telos* within the Christian tradition will be specified in chapter three in the context of a responsive friendship with God manifest in discipleship.

43. Note Hilary Putnam's claim: "We agree with Aristotle that different ideas of human flourishing are appropriate for individuals with different constitutions, but we go further and believe that even in the ideal world there would be different constitutions, that diversity is part of the ideal." *Reason, Truth, and History* (Cambridge: Cambridge University Press, 1981), 148.

44. Amelie O. Rorty suggests something similar in her proposal for a "checks and balances" understanding of the virtues, in which the various virtues both require one another and modify, check and balance, one another. Cf. her "Virtues

and Their Vicissitudes," in *Midwest Studies in Philosophy 13, Ethical Theory: Character and Virtue,* 136–148.

45. The terms are taken from Budziszewski, *Resurrection of Nature,* 71.

46. Augustine's *Confessions* are an excellent example of this twofold process. His conversion leads him to reconstruct the narrative of his life while reorienting his constructive narrative toward the *telos* of communion with God.

47. Richard Bondi, "The Elements of Character," *Journal of Religious Ethics* 12 (1984): 207.

48. A good introduction to the range of Foucault's arguments can be found in *The Foucault Reader,* ed. Paul Rabinow (New York: Pantheon Books, 1984).

49. Fergus Kerr, *Theology After Wittgenstein* (London: Basil Blackwell, 1986), 57.

50. Ludwig Wittgenstein, *Philosophical Investigations,* trans. G. E. M. Anscombe, 3d ed. (New York: MacMillan, 1958), 1.

51. Kerr, *Theology After Wittgenstein,* 59.

52. Ibid., 58.

53. V. N. Voloshinov, *Marxism and the Philosophy of Language* (Cambridge, Mass.: Harvard University Press, 1986). There is considerable debate about the authorship of this book. Many people attribute it to M. K. Bakhtin rather than Voloshinov (who was a colleague of Bakhtin). Happily my use of the argument of this book does not depend on any particular judgments about authorship.

54. Ibid., 94.

55. Ibid., 79–80, 82.

56. The inquiry or challenge can be made by the agent herself.

57. Eric D'Arcy, *Human Acts,* 10.

58. Note that I am describing the physical occurrence in a way that is increasingly event-specific.

59. Kerr, *Theology After Wittgenstein,* 65.

60. Hampshire, *Thought and Action,* 240.

61. Julius Kovesi, *Moral Notions* (London: Routledge and Kegan Paul, 1967).

62. "Table" is an example Kovesi employs. "Coffeepot" is an example Charles Pinches employs in his dissertation "De-

scribing Morally: An Inquiry Concerning the Role of Description in Christian Ethics," University of Notre Dame, 1984. Pinches's dissertation is an extended study of Kovesi's proposal, and I will utilize his analysis in developing my own exposition of Kovesi's work.

63. See Michael Duffey's essay, "The Moral-Nonmoral Distinction in Catholic Ethics: The Sterilization of Moral Language," *Thomist* 49 (1985): 358–59.

64. Kovesi, *Moral Notions*, 24.

65. Ibid., 53.

66. Ibid., 45–46. The use of "anyone" in this passage can be misleading. Kovesi's own point about how moral notions are relative to particular interests and purposes should have cautioned him against the use of a word like "anyone," as will be shown below. I take the reference to mean something like "anyone who is a part of my linguistic community."

67. In what follows I am dependent on Pinches's excellent analysis in "Describing Morally," 78–80.

68. Pinches, "Describing Morally," 79.

69. Ibid., 79–80.

70. Kovesi, *Moral Notions*, 19.

71. Pinches, "Describing Morally," 81.

72. Julius Kovesi, "Descriptions and Reasons," *Proceedings of the Aristotelian Society* 80 (1979–1980): 105.

73. Pinches, "Describing Morally," 83.

74. Voloshinov, *Marxism and the Philosophy of Language*, 106.

75. MacIntyre, *After Virtue*, 187.

76. MacIntyre, "The Intelligibility of Action," 72.

77. Ibid., 75–76.

78. Ibid., 77–78.

79. MacIntyre, *After Virtue*, 186–187.

80. Alasdair MacIntyre, "Positivism, Sociology, and Practical Reasoning: Notes on Durkheim's *Suicide*," in *Human Nature and Natural Knowledge*, ed. A. Donagan, A. N. Perovich, Jr., and M. V. Wedin (Dordrecht: D. Reidel, 1986), 89.

81. Ibid., 96–97.

82. Hence my view differs from that offered by J. Budziszewski, who argues that while an account of the virtues is not "conservative" in some senses of the term, it is

conservative in having a "respectful attitude toward established custom." He concludes that his position offers a theoretical basis for being "moderate," whereas I am arguing that may well—at least in some social orders—be precisely the wrong attitude to take. See J. Budziszewski, *The Nearest Coast of Darkness* (Ithaca, N.Y.: Cornell University Press, 1988), 49–76, especially 76.

83. Alasdair MacIntyre, *Whose Justice? Which Rationality?* (Notre Dame, Ind.: University of Notre Dame Press, 1988).

84. Alan Donagan, *The Theory of Morality* (Chicago: University of Chicago Press, 1977).

85. For an extended critique of Donagan's proposal with which I have great sympathy, see Jeffrey Stout, "Reason and Tradition," chapter 6 of his *Ethics After Babel* (Boston: Beacon Press, 1988).

86. See Walter Lowe, "Barth as a Critic of Dualism: Re-Reading the *Roemerbrief*," *Scottish Journal of Theology* 41 (1988): 377–395.

87. Stout, *Ethics After Babel*, 41. How Stout would characterize "successful moral training" would, however, diverge from my account in important ways.

88. Wittgenstein, *Philosophical Investigations*, 227.

89. Sabina Lovibond, *Realism and Imagination in Ethics* (Minneapolis: University of Minnesota Press, 1983), 32–33.

90. Ibid., 34.

91. See Mark Platts, *Ways of Meaning* (London: Routledge and Kegan Paul, 1979), esp. 261ff. For Lovibond's discussion, see *Realism and Imagination in Ethics*, 31–36.

92. Agnes Heller identifies the relationship between habituated modes of acting, feeling, and thinking on the one hand, and critical reflective thought upon those habituated modes on the other hand, in terms of "repetitive" praxis and thought and "inventive" praxis and thought. See her *Everyday Life* (London: Routledge and Kegan Paul, 1984), esp. 128–133.

93. Aristotle, *Nicomachean Ethics*, trans. Martin Ostwald (Indianapolis, Ind.: Bobbs-Merrill, 1962), 1103a15–18. Further citations will refer to *NE*, and will be made parenthetically in the text.

94. See Nancy Sherman, "Aristotle's Theory of Moral Edu-

cation," Ph.D. dissertation, Harvard University, 1982, and her unpublished paper, "Aristotle's Theory of Moral Habituation." I am greatly indebted to her for my understanding of Aristotle's account of moral formation.

95. Aristotle, *De Anima* 432a22-b7, cited in Nancy Sherman, "Aristotle's Theory of Moral Habituation," 9.

96. Sherman, "Aristotle's Theory of Moral Habituation," 9.

97. For a perspective that fills out this argument in rich and complex ways, see Sara Ruddick, *Maternal Thinking* (Boston: Beacon Press, 1989), esp. 61–123.

98. The phrase is taken from L. A. Kosman's provocative essay "Being Properly Affected: Virtues and Feelings in Aristotle's Ethics," in *Essays on Aristotle's Ethics*, ed. Amelie O. Rorty (Berkeley, Calif.: University of California Press, 1981), 103–116.

99. Kosman, "Being Properly Affected," 112. A similar point is made by Troels Engberg-Pedersen in his *Aristotle's Theory of Moral Insight* (Oxford: Oxford University Press, 1983), 180.

100. See, from a somewhat different perspective, Paul Lauritzen, "Emotions and Religious Ethics," *Journal of Religious Ethics* 16 (1988): 307–324.

101. Sherman, "Aristotle's Theory of Moral Habituation," 16.

102. Hauerwas, *Character and the Christian Life*, xxi-xxii.

103. MacIntyre, *After Virtue*, 149.

104. Heller, *Everyday Life*, 131.

105. I do not mean to suggest that there is any one method or tradition-independent standard of critical reflection. Indeed there are various practices of critical reflective thought. My primary point here is that wise moral judgment includes learning to think well, and such learning entails the practices of reflecting critically on our personal and social lives. For a similar account, see James Tully, "Wittgenstein and Political Philosophy: Understanding Practices of Critical Reflection," *Political Theory* 17 (1989): 172–204.

106. Clodovis Boff, *Theology and Praxis*, trans. Robert R. Barr (Maryknoll, N.Y.: Orbis Books, 1987), 43.

2. Learning to See and Act Rightly

1. MacIntyre, *After Virtue*, 188–189.
2. Ibid., 194.
3. Richard J. Bernstein, "Nietzsche or Aristotle? Reflections on Alasdair MacIntyre's *After Virtue*," *Soundings* 67 (1984): 14.
4. Alasdair MacIntyre, "Bernstein's Distorting Mirrors: A Rejoinder," *Soundings* 67 (1984): 37.
5. MacIntyre, *After Virtue*, 191.
6. Parenting typically involves biological ties, but it need not. Parenting is a vocation that transcends, and is not necessarily bound up with, the biological process of propagating the species. For an important discussion of this point, see Sara Ruddick, *Maternal Thinking* (Boston: Beacon Press, 1989).
7. See Nancy Sherman's "Aristotle's Theory of Moral Education," Ph.D. dissertation, Harvard University, 1982. Though her Aristotelian perspective diverges from my account in important ways both on this specific point and more generally, I am indebted to her work for helping to inform my position. See also my discussion in section 1.3.
8. Robert Wilken, "Alexandria: A School for Training in Virtue," in *Schools of Thought in the Christian Tradition*, ed. Patrick Henry (Philadelphia: Fortress Press, 1984), 21. The internal references are from Gregory Thaumaturgus, *Panegyric* 6:81.
9. Note Ronald Beiner's claim: "To judge is to judge-with, to judge-with is to be a friend. To judge well is a staple of politics. The inference is that friendship is quintessentially political." *Political Judgment* (Chicago: University of Chicago Press, 1983), 82.
10. For example, some spouses meet through a shared practice, but their marriage may become a primary attachment good in itself which is sustained outside of the original practice that occasioned the spouses' meeting.
11. John M. Cooper, "Aristotle on Friendship," in *Essays on Aristotle's Ethics*, ed. Amelie O. Rorty (Berkeley, Calif.: University of California Press, 1981), 329.
12. The image of a "second self" who is a mirror comes from Aristotle's *Magna Moralia* 1213a10–26.

13. I am indebted to Rose Mary Volbrecht's unpublished essay, "Friendship is Particular, but That's OK," 19, for helping me to see this point.

14. MacIntyre, *After Virtue*, 218.

15. Nancy Sherman, "Discerning the Particulars," unpublished paper, 23.

16. This helps to illumine my claim in chapter one that a conception of the *telos* is always partially indeterminate. As people grow, and as they develop a diversity of friends, their vision is extended and deepened and/or challenged and revised, and they begin to see the direction their lives are heading in a new light.

17. The notion of the grammatical account is taken from David Burrell, *Aquinas: God and Action* (Notre Dame, Ind.: University of Notre Dame Press, 1979). The distinction between grammar and description is put to use by Nicholas Lash in his "Considering the Trinity," *Modern Theology* 2 (1986): 294, and in his "Ideology, Metaphor, and Analogy," in *Theology on the Way to Emmaus* (London: SCM Press, 1986), 108–110.

18. Burrell, *Aquinas: God and Action*, 178, n.17.

19. On the dispute between "theism" and "atheism," and the reasons why Christian theology's doctrine of the Trinity dissolves that dispute, see Eberhard Juengel, *God as the Mystery of the World*, trans. Darrell L. Guder (Grand Rapids, Mich.: Wm. B. Eerdmans, 1983). See also Michael J. Buckley, *At the Origins of Modern Atheism* (New Haven, Conn.: Yale University Press, 1988).

20. Lash, *Theology on the Way to Emmaus*, 113.

21. Lash, "Considering the Trinity," 190.

22. Lash, *Theology on the Way to Emmaus*, 113–114.

23. Rowan Williams, "Trinity and Revelation," *Modern Theology* 2 (1986): 208.

24. For an interesting and provocative account linking the depiction of God as Triune to the shaping of Christian life, see Vigen Guroian, "Love in Orthodox Ethics: Trinitarian and Christological Reflections," in *Incarnate Love* (Notre Dame, Ind.: University of Notre Dame Press, 1987), 29–48.

25. Lash, "Considering the Trinity," 193.

26. See James M. Gustafson, *Ethics from a Theocentric Per-*

spective, vols. I and II (Chicago: University of Chicago Press, 1981 and 1984). Gustafson's work is interesting for the similarities with, and differences from, the argument developed in this book. In many of his writings he has argued for the importance of the agent's perspective, for the centrality of social contexts in understanding the moral life, and for the interrelation between moral education and moral judgment. His constructive account embodies the conviction that depictions of God, the world, and life and death significantly shape an account of ethics and moral judgment. But there are significant differences between his theological perspective and mine; hence, as the argument of this book should suggest, there are also significant differences between his account of ethics and moral judgment and mine.

27. Lash, *Theology on the Way to Emmaus*, 154–155. See also his *Easter in Ordinary* (Charlottesville, Va.: University Press of Virginia, 1988).

28. Lash's most complete account is found in *Easter in Ordinary*, 266–272. Earlier versions of the argument can be found in "Considering the Trinity," 193–194, and in *Theology on the Way to Emmaus*, 155–156.

29. Lash, *Easter in Ordinary*, 267.

30. Ibid., 268.

31. Ibid.

32. Ibid., 269.

33. Ibid., 270.

34. Ibid., 271.

35. A similar construal of the Trinity is provided by Leonardo Boff in his *Trinity and Society*, trans. Paul Burns (Maryknoll, N.Y.: Orbis Books, 1988).

36. Lash, *Theology on the Way to Emmaus*, 156.

37. Mary Midgley, *Beast and Man* (Ithaca, N.Y.: Cornell University Press, 1978).

38. On this point, see also Nicholas Lash's analysis of William James's account of religious experience in *Easter in Ordinary*.

39. Lash, *Easter in Ordinary*, 255.

40. Elaine Scarry's *The Body in Pain* (Oxford: Oxford University Press, 1985) contains brilliant discussions of the unmaking and making of the world and the precarious nature

of human identity and personhood in relation to such destruction and construction.

41. Lash, *Theology on the Way to Emmaus*, 153.

42. I am indebted to Juergen Moltmann, *The Passion for Life*, trans. M. Douglas Meeks (Philadelphia: Fortress Press, 1978), 56, for seeing the significance of this passage for discussion about friendship with God.

43. David Burrell, "The Spirit and the Christian Life," in *Christian Theology*, ed. Peter C. Hodgson and Robert H. King (Philadelphia: Fortress Press, 1982), 248.

44. Thomas Aquinas, *Compendium Theologiae*, 226, found in *Theological Texts*, ed. Thomas Gilby (Durham, N.C.: Labyrinth Press, 1982), 311. Emphasis added.

45. See Thomas Aquinas, *Summa Theologica*, trans. Fathers of the English Dominican Province (New York: Benziger Brothers, 1948), I-II q. 109, a. 5. Hereafter cited as *ST*.

46. "[God's] giving of grace issues from great friendship, yes, the greatest ..." Exposition, *St. John*, iii, *lect.* 3, found in *Theological Texts*, 281.

47. Thomas Aquinas, *Compendium Theologiae*, 226, found in *Theological Texts*, 310.

48. *ST* III q. 48, a. 2, ad. 1. It is unclear precisely how to take the reference to "satisfaction." One ought to be careful about making too quick a connection to Anselm's doctrine; while there are certainly similarities between Thomas's language and Anselm's doctrine, to draw Anselmian conclusions would raise a host of questions which Thomas does not address systematically.

49. *ST* III q. 46, a. 3.

50. *ST* III q. 26, a. 1.

51. I am indebted to Paul Wadell for helping me see this connection in Thomas's thought. See Wadell's "Charity as Friendship With God and Form of the Virtues," Ph.D. dissertation, University of Notre Dame, 1984, 439. More generally I am indebted to Wadell for pointing me to significant passages in Thomas's thought.

52. *ST* III q. 75, a. 1.

53. *ST* III q. 73, a. 1.

54. Ibid. It is significant that Thomas describes charity as "friendship with God." Thus Thomas's phrase could be re-

worded in his own terms to say that the eucharist is "the sacrament of friendship with God."

55. Thomas Aquinas, *IV Sentences*, x.I, found in *Theological Texts*, 367.

56. *ST* III q. 75, a. 1, found in *Theological Texts*, 368.

57. *ST* III q. 73, a. 3, ad. 2.

58. *ST* III q. 79, a. 4, ad. 1.

59. *ST* III q. 79, a. 6.

60. *ST* III q. 79, a. 2.

61. *ST* II-II q. 23, a. 1.

62. *ST* I-II q. 65, a. 5. The reference to Aristotle is from Book VIII, 2,12 (1155b28; 1161b11).

63. *ST* II-II q. 23, a. 1.

64. *ST* II-II q. 24, a. 2.

65. Fergus Kerr provides an interesting discussion of Thomas on the issue of charity as friendship. See "Charity as Friendship," *Language, Meaning and God*, ed. Brian Davies (London: Geoffrey Chapman, 1988), 1–23.

66. Jeremy Taylor, cited in Gilbert Meilaender, *Friendship* (Notre Dame, Ind.: University of Notre Dame Press, 1981), 1.

67. See Anders Nygren, *Agape and Eros*, trans. Philip S. Watson (Philadelphia: Westminster Press, 1953); Gene Outka, *Agape* (New Haven, Conn.: Yale University Press, 1972).

68. Though he operates with a slightly different understanding of *agape* and friendship than I do, and though he does not discuss Thomas directly, Meilaender's *Friendship* contains a rich discussion of these issues.

69. Helen Oppenheimer, *The Hope of Happiness* (London: SCM Press, 1983), 131.

70. *ST* III, Prologue.

71. Ibid.

72. *ST* II-II q. 184, a. 2.

73. E. Thurneysen, *The Sermon on the Mount* (Richmond, Va.: John Knox Press, 1964), 71, cited in John Webster, "Christology, Imitability, and Ethics," *Scottish Journal of Theology* 39 (1985): 312. Though I dissent from some of his exegesis and his conclusions about the relationship between Christology and imitability, I am indebted to Webster's article for helping me see the context of Protestant fears about the language of imitation.

74. Otto Weber, *Foundations of Dogmatics I* (Grand Rapids, Mich.: Wm. B. Eerdmans, 1983), 322, cited in Webster, "Christology, Imitability, and Ethics," 317.

75. I am indebted to Gil Meilaender for this way of formulating the issue.

76. Williams, "Trinity and Revelation," 202.

77. Oliver O'Donovan, *Resurrection and Moral Order* (Grand Rapids, Mich.: Wm. B. Eerdmans, 1986), 224.

78. Of course, to the extent that those friendships and practices are corrupted and/or distorted there will be a malformation rather than a formation.

79. Horace Bushnell, *Christian Nurture* (Grand Rapids, Mich.: Baker Book House, 1979), 10.

80. See Webster, "Christology, Imitability, and Ethics," *passim*, particularly 310–311.

81. Stephen Fowl, "Some Uses of Story in Paul's Moral Discourse," *Modern Theology* 4 (1988): 304.

82. Karl Barth, *Church Dogmatics IV/2*, trans. Geoffrey Bromiley (Edinburgh: T. and T. Clark, 1958), 513. I am indebted to Kenneth Surin for directing me to this passage.

3. Learning to Live in the Mystery
of the Triune God

1. Williams, "Trinity and Revelation," 201.

2. Ibid.

3. Rowan Williams, *Resurrection* (New York: Pilgrim Press, 1982), 84.

4. On the importance of communal dialogue patterned in the Trinity, see also Boff, *Trinity and Society*, 120.

5. Williams, "Trinity and Revelation," 206.

6. Ray S. Anderson, *Historical Transcendence and the Reality of God* (London: Geoffrey Chapman, 1976), 233.

7. He critiques such theologians as Walter Kasper, Juergen Moltmann, Eberhard Juengel, and Wolfhart Pannenberg. See John Milbank, "The Second Difference," *Modern Theology* 2 (1986): 213–234.

8. Ibid., 216.

9. Ibid., 230.

10. Ibid., 228.

11. Indeed the logic of Paul's argument seems to suggest that the language of "individual" would make no sense if abstracted from its connection to community. For an interesting discussion of Paul along these lines, albeit cast in "idealistic" terms, see Josiah Royce, *The Problem of Christianity* (Chicago: University of Chicago Press, 1918).

12. Leonardo Boff provides an interesting and more complete discussion of this in *Trinity and Society*.

13. See Anderson, *Historical Transcendence and the Reality of God, passim,* esp. 232, 250.

14. Williams, *Resurrection,* 71.

15. Ibid., 89.

16. Ibid., 42.

17. The difficulty with the formulations of the Holy Spirit's work which stress that the one Spirit perfectly operative in Jesus Christ is also operative in the Church is that it renders such puzzlement problematic, when in fact puzzlement is precisely what characterizes the ongoing life of the Church. Walter Kasper's otherwise excellent *The God of Jesus Christ* (New York: Crossroad, 1984) is an example of such a conception of the Holy Spirit.

18. Williams, "Trinity and Revelation," 207–208.

19. James William McClendon, *Ethics: Systematic Theology* vol. I (Nashville, Tenn.: Abingdon Press, 1986), 221. Thanks to Michael G. Cartwright for reminding me of this passage.

20. See particularly Mikhail Bakhtin, *Problems of Dostoevsky's Poetics,* trans. Caryl Emerson (Minneapolis, Minn.: University of Minnesota Press, 1984).

21. Boff, *Trinity and Society,* 107.

22. I have been helped in my understanding of the relationship between Christian practices and Christian community by Terry Tilley's review essay, "Why American Catholic Theologians Should Read 'baptist' Theology," *Horizons* 14 (1987): 129–137, and by an exchange of letters between Tilley and James McClendon (whose work is the focus of the review essay).

23. For a good discussion of these matters, see Gerhard Lohfink, *Jesus and Community* (Philadelphia: Fortress Press, 1984). George Lindbeck touches on these matters in his "The

Story-Shaped Church," in *Scriptural Authority and Narrative Interpretation*, ed. Garrett Green (Philadelphia: Fortress Press, 1987), 161–178.

24. I am using the language of "Christian community" rather than "Church" for several reasons. First, my emphasis is on the *practices* of community rather than the institutions that house those practices, and "Church" denotes both the practices and the institutions. Second, "Church" is sometimes used to refer to particular denominational bodies (e.g., the United Methodist *Church*) in a way that seems to obscure rather than clarify its intended reference (e.g., it confuses the part for the whole). Third, there is a history of issues surrounding what constitutes "the Church" about which I will not be concerned except tangentially; for example, I will not concern myself with distinctions between the "visible" and "invisible" Church because my focus on community will presuppose concrete and historical relationships.

25. This term is less than adequate, for it generally refers to particular groups within Protestantism. I am using it to describe not only those groups conventionally designated as "denominations" but three others as well: Roman Catholics, Eastern Orthodox (in all their internal diversity), and those who identify themselves as "non-denominational" and/or "interdenominational" Protestants.

26. Although I cannot argue the point here, it seems to me that this largely describes our current situation, at least in the "First World" of Euro-American Christianity. For a cogent description of our social situation, the ways in which it infects local congregations, and the communal strategies needed to deal with our situation, see Kenneth Surin, "*Contemptus Mundi* and the Disenchantment of the World," *Journal of the American Academy of Religion* 53 (1985): 383–410.

27. Though the story is complex, this is in part what happened with the Wesleyan class meetings in England. What started out as Christian communities more restricted in scope than local congregations (i.e., those in the class meetings participated in local Anglican parishes and only there received the sacraments) eventually developed into institutionally defined and denominationally identified congregations.

28. This is a matter that cannot be resolved *a priori*; it

requires either (in the case of a third party) ethnographic analysis of the practices as the community describes them and as they are employed in the communities, or (in the case of the two communities) conversation about the similarities and differences between them—conversation being itself an important and worthwhile practice which fosters particular kinds of community.

29. Stephen Sykes develops the idea (borrowing a phrase from W. B. Gallie) of Christianity as "an essentially contested concept" in his *The Identity of Christianity* (Philadelphia: Fortress Press, 1984), *passim*, esp. 251ff. The reference is to Gallie's *Philosophy and Historical Understanding* (London: Chatto and Windus, 1964).

30. The use of "all" in this sentence is obviously question-begging. For there is no practice that is central to the self-definition of every community or person who lays claim to being Christian (e.g., the Quakers do not practice baptism or eucharist). While a full discussion of the issue would take me far afield, I would claim that—for reasons crucial to the argument of this chapter—those communities and persons who do not embody the "central" Christian practices of baptism, eucharist, forgiveness-reconciliation, and the interpretation of Scripture (or who have a widely divergent view of what constitutes Scripture) are to that extent deficient in their view of what being Christian entails.

31. This distinction is drawn from Tilley, "Why American Catholic Theologians Should Read 'baptist' Theology."

32. Though, of course, they cannot exist for long without developing some relation to "institutions," as MacIntyre notes (see *After Virtue*, 194). The point is that the relationship between these practices and institutions is fundamentally different from "institutionally bound" practices, and that hence it is crucial that we not collapse the distinction between practices and institutions.

33. That I even describe level three of Christian community and think it to be of crucial importance in our culture is a reflection of my conviction that the rehabilitation, renewal, and reformation of Christian practices is an ongoing task.

34. These disagreements are reflective of the ongoing puzzlement over how best we can imitate Christ. So, for exam-

ple, if I belong to a community which baptizes selectively, baptizing only those who profess faith (i.e., "believers' baptism"), my puzzlement may be how a symbol of acceptance (adoption, inclusion) that focuses on the priority of God's action is seen to operate as a symbol of exclusion, stipulating human conditions that must be satisfied before acceptance is possible; conversely, if I belong to a community which baptizes relatively "indiscriminately," baptizing infants and others who are incapable of responding (i.e., "infant baptism"), my puzzlement may be how a symbol of commitment (immersion, initiation) has become divorced from its natural function in relation to a visible and continuous belonging to a particular group. I owe this example to Rowan Williams, "Trinity and Revelation," 207.

35. Juergen Moltmann has suggested that the most apt description for the Church is a "community of friends." See his *The Church in the Power of the Spirit* (New York: Harper and Row, 1977), esp. 316–317.

36. See, in addition to the Romans passage, 1 Cor. 1:13; 10:2; 12:13; Gal. 3:27. I am indebted to Stephen Fowl's "Some Uses of Story in Moral Discourse" for showing the relation of these passages to Paul's argument in Romans 6.

37. Ibid., 297.

38. Williams, *Resurrection*, 61.

39. This is a point made by Robert Jenson in his *The Triune Identity* (Philadelphia: Fortress Press, 1982).

40. MacIntyre, *After Virtue*, 216.

41. Theodore Jennings puts the point well when in discussing the importance of ritual action (of which baptism is a significant Christian example) he says, "Ritual knowledge is gained through a bodily action which alters the world or the place of the ritual participant in the world." Jennings, "On Ritual Knowledge," *Journal of Religion* 62 (1982): 115.

42. It is because of this second focus of baptism that whenever new persons are baptized into the community, those already baptized still participate in the practice—albeit in a different way—by "remembering their baptism."

43. Williams, *Resurrection*, 62.

44. Fredric Jameson, "On Magic Realism in Film," *Critical Inquiry* 12 (1986): 304, cited in Kenneth Surin, *The Turnings of*

Darkness and Light (Cambridge: Cambridge University Press, 1989), 217.

45. The reference is to Julia Kristeva, "From One Identity to An Other," in her *Desire in Language: A Semiotic Approach to Language and Art,* ed. L. S. Roudiez (Oxford: Blackwell, 1981), 124–147, cited in Surin, *The Turnings of Darkness and Light,* 217.

46. Surin, *The Turnings of Darkness and Light,* 217.

47. John Chrysostom, "Homily XXV, 3 on Matthew," cited in Geoffrey Wainwright, "Eucharist and/as Ethics," unpublished manuscript, 5.

48. Williams, *Resurrection,* 109.

49. Geoffrey Wainwright, *Eucharist and Eschatology* (New York: Oxford University Press, 1971), 82.

50. For a profound meditation on the relationship between the crucifixion, estrangement, and friendship, see Sebastian Moore, *The Crucified Jesus is No Stranger* (Minneapolis, Minn.: Seabury Press, 1977).

51. Williams, *Resurrection,* 91–92.

52. The degree to which eucharistic practice should be "open" or "closed" is another of the ongoing puzzles of Christian community. The structure of the issue is analogous to the question of indiscriminate and selective practice of baptism (note 34); hence it is imperative to remember that both views recollect important features of Jesus' ministry which need to be held in creative tension rather than adopting an either/or. Here the main point in stressing the "openness" of the eucharist is to be a reminder that we do not *choose* with whom we will sit at the table; the fellowship of the table is established by Christ.

53. Williams, *Resurrection,* 70.

54. Ibid., 114.

55. These terms are borrowed from Dietrich Bonhoeffer, *The Communion of Saints,* trans. R. Gregor Smith (New York: Harper and Row, 1963).

56. Pierre-Yves Emery, *The Communion of Saints,* trans. D. J. and M. Watson (New York: Morehouse-Barlow, 1966), 226. Elsewhere he writes, "Now this communion always includes a fellowship in expectation: if the Eucharist makes us share

in advance in the feast of heaven and the joy of the saints, it reminds us as well—and we say so to God—that the saints await us and wish to see us sharers in their sanctity and their joy" (210).

57. Robert Imbelli, "Toward a Catholic Vision: The Theology of the Communion of Saints," *Review for Religious* (1983): 295.

58. That Christians participate in a variety of communities is a reminder that, while forgiveness-reconciliation is a central practice of Christian community, it is also an indispensable virtue to be embodied in individual believers.

59. James William McClendon, Jr., *Ethics: Systematic Theology* vol. I, 229–230.

60. See Jenson, *The Triune Identity*, for an extended discussion of this point.

61. Colin Gunton provides a suggestive, though incomplete, account of the connection between the unity-in-diversity of Scripture and the unity-in-diversity of the Triune God in his *Enlightenment and Alienation* (Grand Rapids, Mich.: Wm. B. Eerdmans, 1985). I think a complete account would, however, need to develop a more dynamic understanding of the relationship between Scripture and Christian community than Gunton seems to think is necessary.

62. See Lindbeck, *The Nature of Doctrine*, 117–118.

63. This is Stanley Hauerwas's suggested revision of the claim that Scripture "creates" a world in his *A Community of Character* (Notre Dame, Ind.: University of Notre Dame Press, 1981), 57.

64. Williams, *Resurrection*, 72.

65. Though not traditionally described as a virtue, cruciformity is indispensable. In one sense it is a comprehensive description of a life patterned in Christ, but in the sense I am using it here it describes the virtue of "allowing the truth to be embodied in one's life."

66. This is a difficult matter, for clearly suffering is in itself neither a skill nor a virtue. Because Christian discipleship is patterned in Jesus Christ, however, it is essential to recognize that the ways in which suffering is to be borne do require skill and virtue. Hence I have adopted the language of "obedient suffering."

67. Lash, "Performing the Scriptures," in *Theology on the Way to Emmaus*, 37–46.

68. Ibid., 42.

69. Ibid., 43.

70. It needs to be remembered, however, that priority is still to be given to the performer, not to the scholar or critic.

71. Lash, *Theology on the Way to Emmaus*, 43.

72. Often translated as practical wisdom, *phronesis* carries the sense of a discerning and wise moral judgment.

73. The importance of communal *phronesis* for interpreting and performing Scripture has been noted in Lewis S. Mudge, "Toward an Ecclesial Hermeneutic," in *Formation and Reflection*, ed. Lewis S. Mudge and James N. Poling (Philadelphia: Fortress Press, 1987), 114, as well as in Stephen Fowl, "Some Uses of Story in Moral Discourse," 15–16. A more complete discussion is provided by John Howard Yoder in "The Hermeneutics of Peoplehood," in *The Priestly Kingdom* (Notre Dame, Ind.: University of Notre Dame Press, 1984), 15–45.

74. Robert Wilken has powerfully shown how the "Alexandrian school" in early Christianity, to which I briefly adverted in chapter two, had as its focus the formation of Christian character. The primary means by which people learned to interpret Scripture and learned what it means to be a Christian were by being befriended by members of the community (such as Origen) seen to be persons of practical wisdom. See Wilken, "Alexandria: A School for Training in Virtue," in *Schools of Thought in the Christian Tradition*, 15–30.

75. Surin, *The Turnings of Darkness and Light*, 219.

76. Imbelli, "Toward a Catholic Vision," 291.

Conclusion

1. For an interesting and penetrating discussion of the issue, see Fredric Jameson, "On Habits of the Heart," *South Atlantic Quarterly* 86 (1987): 545–565.

2. Martin Buber, *I and Thou*, trans. Walter Kaufman (Edinburgh: T. and T. Clark, 1970), 156.

INDEX

185